BIBLE REFLECTIONS

Inductive Study

Allison Light

WESTBOW
PRESS®
A DIVISION OF THOMAS NELSON
& ZONDERVAN

WestBow Press books may be ordered through booksellers or by contacting:

WestBow Press
A Division of Thomas Nelson & Zondervan
1663 Liberty Drive
Bloomington, IN 47403
www.westbowpress.com
1 (866) 928-1240

ISBN: 978-1-5127-6153-5 (sc)
ISBN: 978-1-5127-6154-2 (hc)
ISBN: 978-1-5127-6152-8 (e)

Library of Congress Control Number: 2016917415

Print information available on the last page.

WestBow Press rev. date: 11/11/2016

Dedication

I could not have completed this book without
assistance from Jesus Christ
and
my understanding husband

CONTENTS

FOREWORD

I'm so glad you are choosing to read this book. It's exciting to contemplate the awakening of your greater understanding of The Bible and our Triune God. It's wonderful to envision your closer walk with Him. This book is written expressly to assist you in your own Bible study. You will see footnoted texts for further study. These texts will bring better understanding and assist you to make this Bible study personally yours.

Points to assist you:

- Choose to use an authorized translation of Scripture.
- Choose one that you find easy to read. Some love the King James Version (KJV) or you might prefer the New International Version (NIV). Both are accurate and a good choice. The NIV is a thorough translation of the original text with easy readability which, in my opinion, maintains the cadence of the King James Version. I became very familiar with King James when, as a child, I memorized many of its passages. I still return to it today to aid in my own study and to find difficult passages. One point regarding the NIV, which I find less appealing, is that not all of the texts which appear in the King James are in the body of the NIV; instead certain texts appear as footnotes.
- You can look up the Scriptures in King James, New King James American Standard, Douay or other legitimate, authorized texts and you will arrive at the same conclusion.
- You can look up texts on your electronic media e.g. Bible Gateway, etc.
- As you read through this book, note that pronouns which refer to God—as well as any of His names—are always capitalized. This is my way of showing respect and deference for our Sovereign Creator.
- When you see, in Scripture, a reference to "saint" or "the saints," understand that these are NOT individuals canonized by a church. Saints, as referenced in Scripture, are all people who love The Lord God and have made Jesus Christ the Lord of their lives.
- When looking up texts, "ff" following a text means to read the verse indicated and the verses which follow.
- You will find a listing of books of The Bible with corresponding abbreviations as used in this study, see page x.

- The book abbreviation refers to all chapters and verses which follow until the next book is noted (e.g. Ps. 40:11; 103:2-4; Lam. 3:22-23).
- Chapters are separated by semi-colon (;)
- Verses are separated by comma (,)
- A thought may be footnoted with a corresponding text at the bottom of the page. These are listed for your additional study. I hope you will take advantage of these texts to widen your knowledge and to allow the facts to truly become your own.
- A footnote entry of "Ibid" refers to the last reference in the immediately preceding footnote.
- The designation of "Lp" following a verse means the passage referred to is in the last part of the verse, eg.1Sam. 15:22Lp.
- This study guide does not offer a text, tell you what to believe about that text and then ask you to re-state the information given, to ensure that you do in fact agree with the author's commentary or interpretation.
- This is an inductive study; that is, you look up the texts indicated and allow The Holy Spirit to show you truth through the weight of Scriptural evidence.
- I will never ask you to take my word for truth; but I do ask you to prayerfully study the passages given—and other passages you find as you study Scripture.
- The questions at the end of each section are for your learning and self-evaluation. I hope you will take the time to answer them—they will aid in your spiritual growth.
- Always begin each Bible study with prayer for God to guide you into all truth.
- The best instructor is The Holy Spirit of God as you read and study The Bible, which is the infallible, inerrant Word of God.
- Do not be afraid to mark or write in your Bible. This is one way in which you become familiar with texts. The Word of God becomes personal to you and you will find texts more rapidly.
- Write notes in the margin of your Bible to describe how a text was meaningful in a situation.
- Note any promises you have claimed (e.g. "claimed, Nov. 25, 2016"); then, remember to revisit the passage in the future to note how and when God answered a prayer, etc.
- I invite you to grab a notebook and a pen and embark on this exciting study of the attributes of our wonderful Triune God.

BOOKS OF THE BIBLE WITH CORRESPONDING ABBREVIATIONS AS USED IN THIS STUDY GUIDE

Old Testament
39 Books

New Testament
27 Books

Genesis	Gen.	Ecclesiastes	Eccl.	Matthew	Mt.	1 Peter	1Pet.
Exodus	Ex.	Song of Solomon	SS.	Mark	Mk.	2 Peter	2Pet.
Leviticus	Lev.	Isaiah	Isa.	Luke	Lk.	1 John	1Jn.
Numbers	Num.	Jeremiah	Jer.	John	Jn.	2 John	2Jn.
Deuteronomy	Deut.	Lamentation	Lam.	Acts	Ac.	3 John	3Jn.
Joshua	Jos.	Ezekiel	Ezk.	Romans	Rom.	Jude	Jude
Judges	Judg.	Daniel	Dan.	1 Corinthians	1Cor.	Revelation	Rev.
Ruth	Ru.	Hosea	Hos.	2 Corinthians	2Cor.		
1 Samuel	1Sam.	Joel	Jol.	Galatians	Gal.		
2 Samuel	2Sam.	Amos	Ams.	Ephesians	Eph.		
1 Kings	1Ki.	Obadiah	Obd.	Philippians	Php.		
2 Kings	2Ki.	Jonah	Jnh.	Colossians	Col.		
1 Chronicles	1Chr.	Micah	Mic.	1Thessalonians	1Th.		
2 Chronicles	2Chr.	Nahum	Nah.	2Thessalonians	2Th.		
Ezra	Ezr.	Habakkuk	Hbk.	1 Timothy	1Tim.		
Nehemiah	Neh.	Zephaniah	Zep.	2 Timothy	2Tim.		
Esther	Est.	Haggai	Hag.	Titus	Tts.		
Job	Job	Zechariah	Zec.	Philemon	Phlm.		
Psalm	Ps.	Malachi	Mal.	Hebrews	Heb.		
Proverbs	Prov.			James	Jas.		

TRUTH

Truth seems to have reached the societal age of relativity—it has become a state of mind. Truth, by man's standards, can be anything one wants it to be.

Man purports to be in search of truth. Professors are teaching their ideas of truth as dictated by the Federal Government via the Education Association. Professors feel wise and very important as they discuss the philosophies of Darwin's evolution and various world religions including Pantheism, Monotheism, Deism and Agnosticism. They will study Plato and Voltaire, as well as many other philosophies; but professors are very loath to answer questions or discuss the Christian religion and specifically, Jesus Christ. It really is a case of the blind leading the blind.

They say they are in search of truth, but they refuse to study the One who is Truth.[1] Our founding fathers provided for freedom from religion, to ensure that government could not force a state religion on the masses. Our judicial system has warped that statement to be separation of church and state. Initially this meant that the state could not mandate church practice. This has been further skewed to mean Christianity cannot be brought into the public sector. Now, separation of church and state as federally mandated, specifically means: no public discussion or display of Jesus Christ and Christianity.

Do you wonder why every other religion, along with its gods, is welcomed into the classroom—but not Christianity and Jesus Christ? We should not be surprised. Jesus wasn't welcome in the world He created; nor by the people He created.[2] This same mandate was given to Jesus' disciples when they were brought before the Sanhedrin for preaching the Gospel. They were told not to speak or preach in the Name of Jesus.[3] Today, we can blame ourselves for this current state of affairs. Christians have been lackadaisical and downright inattentive or uncaring of events as they have unfolded. We are like the proverbial frog contentedly sitting in the water as it gets warmer and warmer—the water is reaching the boiling point!

[1] Ps. 43:3;145:1; 119:30;Jn. 14:6;2Th.2:10Lp;
[2] 1Jn. 1:6; 8:31-32; Phl. 4:8; 2Tim.3:16
[3] Ac, 4:16,17

Satan hasn't had a new bag of tricks since the beginning of time. I guess he doesn't need a new one. Apparently the old one is working well enough. People have an increasingly warped sense of truth. God said before the end of time, people will love lies more than truth. They will call evil good and good evil.[4] I can see that happening now. Can you?

We are blessed to have the infallible, inerrant Word of Almighty God. Forty Holy men of God spoke this Word as they were moved by the Holy Spirit. Moses wrote the first five books over 3500 years ago and John wrote the last book over 1900 years ago. God is more than able to preserve His Word and these Scriptures bring wisdom and prepare us to instruct and teach all righteousness. This is the textbook that should be used for counseling members of our congregations. What could be better counsel than that obtained from God's Word?

God's Word is relevant for healing marriages, rearing children, race relations, family and interpersonal relationships, work place behavior and health, to name only a few important areas. Why would we choose the counsel of the world when we can have counsel from Almighty God? Surely, He transcends any counsel we could obtain from the world.

> Thy Word have I hidden in my heart
> So that I won't sin against You.[5]
> Thy word is a lamp unto my feet
> And a light for my path[6]
> Sanctify us by Your Truth
> Thy Word is Truth[7]

---

[4] Isa. 5:20,21; Jn. 3:19
[5] Ps. 119:11
[6] Ps. 119:105
[7] Jn. 17:17

Truth Revisited

1. Did you take time to check out the study texts?
   ___ All ___ Some ___ None

2. Have you been aware that leaders in the government and professors in education are attempting to stifle the Truth of God? Yes___ No___

3. Are you concerned about what your children are learning in school? Yes___ No___

4. Do you believe it is important for Christians to stand up for Bible truth?

5. Do you believe God's Word is infallible? Yes ___ No___

6. Do you have a reliably translated copy of God's Word? Yes ___ No___

7. Do you make reading The Bible a priority? Yes___ No___

8. Do you read it with your spouse? Yes ___ No ___

9. Do you read it with the children? Yes___ No___

10. Have you always exercised your God-given right to vote?

11. Keeping in mind that no one is perfect, do you vote for the candidate who most nearly represents God's standards?

12. What does this text from Romans 3:4 mean to you?
    "Let God be true and every man a liar."

_____

_____

PRAYER

Prayer Preparation

In order to pray effectively, one must know The Scriptures. If you are not reading your Bible, get started today! We do not know how to pray if we don't know God's Word. God's Word is alive and active and sharper than a double-edged sword.[1] Passages come alive as we read them and they speak to us. If you have ever desired for God to speak to you, read The Bible. Much of what He says to us comes straight out of Scripture. Many times the answer to your questions will jump right off the page as you read Scripture and pray. Another reason for knowing God's Word is because we need to pray God's Word back to Him. Our words tend to be empty and, many times, meaningless—we just do not know how to pray; but God's Word never comes back empty.[2] As you read The Word of God, be prepared for a life-adventure, as He speaks to you and as you proceed in obedience.

God tells us to put on the "armor of God" so we can stand against the devil's schemes.[3] You and I often see struggles and heartaches caused by humans, but The Bible says our struggle is not against flesh and blood but against rulers, authorities and powers of this dark world and spiritual forces of evil in the heavenly realms. This heavenly realm is our world's heaven or firmament.[4] This is not the heaven where Satan attended God's staff meetings.[5] Since Jesus died on the cross, Satan has no access to the third heaven, where God's throne and court reside. The heavenly realm where there is spiritual warfare is our firmament where birds fly and where we conduct space travel. The prophet Daniel alluded to this activity when he told of a time when an angel came to answer his prayer.[6] We often focus on the individual through whom we see testing come; but fail to recognize that unseen forces, holy and unholy are at work in all of creation, for good or evil.[7]

---

[1] Heb. 4:12
[2] Isa. 55:11; Jer. 1:12
[3] Eph. 6:10ff
[4] Gen. 1:6
[5] Job 1:6ff;2:1ff
[6] Dan. 10:1-21 (especially vss.12-13,21)
[7] Rom. 8:19-22

Perhaps you wonder why God first tells us to put on the belt of truth and then the breast plate of righteousness. It seems as if we are getting dressed out-of-order. Any preparation for service must begin with truth, which moves us toward righteousness. Righteousness moves us to speak The Gospel of Peace, which increases our faith and faith makes us sure in our salvation. All of these pieces work together to prepare us to find The Word of God an indispensable part of our armor. We read The Word of God and meditate on it; but we are not ready to wield it as part of our armor until the other systems are in place.

The last part of the passage admonishes us to pray in the Spirit on all occasions—that means praying throughout the day. We are unable to pray in the Spirit unless we know The Word of God. The Spirit speaks through God's Word. The passage goes on to tell us to pray with all kinds of prayer (praise, thanksgiving, worship, submission, requests, anguish—all kinds).

Prayer Warrior, armored soldier, angel, serpent

Jesus tells us to make requests of Him boldly[8] because He is willing and eager to supply all of our needs.

---

[8] Heb. 4:16; Phil 4:19

I can't tell you how many times individuals have said to me, "Oh I pray for other people; but I never pray for myself—that would be selfish" or "I don't want to bother Him about me." This is an example of false humility. We must obey God who tells us to ask for whatever we need.[9] He also tells us through the Apostle James that we don't have because we either don't ask or, having asked, we don't receive because we ask with wrong motives[10] and for our own pleasure. How can we ask with pure and right motives unless we know God's Word? It is through His Word that He makes known His will to us. As an encouragement to you, let me remind you that when we pray sincerely but do not know how to pray, The Holy Spirit of Jesus comes along side and corrects our prayer and prays it for us, according to God's will.[11] Doesn't it just bless you to know that God does that for us?!

The Armor of God

Remember, God commands that once the armor is in place, we are to STAND FIRM![12]

What	Where	Function
Belt of Truth	Waist	To protect personal integrity & protect from falsehoods
Breast Plate of Righteousness	Chest	Protect cardio-pulmonary health & maintain a spiritually faithful heart
Shoes of The Gospel of Peace	Feet	Ready to proclaim The Gospel of Jesus in season or out of season—when people want to hear it and when they do not[13]
Shield of Faith	Hand	Extinguish the flaming darts of the evil one—the attacks of Satan
Helmet of Salvation	Head	Protection of mind & brain; to protect us physically & spiritually
Sword of the Spirit	Head, Mind, Tongue	This is The Word of God to pierce darkness & boldly, gently & with respect give a reason for hope within us[14]

---

[9] Mt. 7:7,8
[10] Jas. 4:2,3
[11] Rom. 8:26,27
[12] Eph. 6:13,14
[13] 2Tim. 4:2; 1Pet 3:15
[14] Ibid; Isa. 52:7; Rom 10:14,15

Pray Without Ceasing

This is the prayer you pray while you are engaged in the activities of life. Perhaps while spreading The Gospel, gardening, shopping, disciplining children, making love to your spouse, driving, teaching a class, playing, working and on all other occasions: happy, fearful, terrifying. Pray without ceasing. You don't have to wait until you are kneeling at church, have candles burning or any other special thing—you just need to have a heart tuned into God. Perhaps you like to enjoy the clouds, walk on the beach and watch your children; all while talking to God and thanking Him. If you pray without ceasing you will follow The Bible mandate to live at peace with all people, in so far as it depends upon you.[15]

There will be no time for gossip, coveting, stealing, lying, adultery or other things contrary to God's law. There is no place that God doesn't hear our prayers. I had a friend tell me that she often sits on the toilet and prays and reads The Bible because it's quiet and she can be undisturbed. Whatever works for you will work for God. He just loves to have His children talk to Him. Instead of finding fault and criticizing, you will view people as in need of Jesus Christ. Remember that God doesn't see people the way you and I do.[16] Let our prayer be that God will give us His eyes to see as He sees, His heart to understand as He understands, His hands to touch as His would touch and our mouths to speak as He would speak. Ask Jesus to help your heart break with those things that break His heart and your heart to rejoice with those things that cause His heart to rejoice. If you tend to have a downcast-appearing face, ask God to give you a joyful heart that is evident in your face, with a smile on your lips, in your voice and in your eyes.[17]

Phoniness is obvious to those with whom we minister. In business we are often told to answer the phone smiling, because the smile is heard in our voice and reflects positively on the company. Well, let's reflect positively for The Gospel of Jesus Christ by letting the world see and hear us as joyful, cheerful Christians. We are, after all, ambassadors for Christ.[18]

---

[15] Rom. 12:18
[16] 1Sam. 16:7
[17] Prov. 15:13; 17:22
[18] 2Cor. 5:20

Pray Praise

> Our Father, who art in Heaven, hallowed be Thy Name.
> Thy Kingdom come;
> Thy will be done on earth as it is in Heaven.[19]

We are addressing our adored, revered and worshipped Father. His address and His throne are in Heaven. We are acknowledging that He is holy—His very Name is holy.[20] We are telling Him that we eagerly await His return to this earth to put an end to sin. In the meantime, we are inviting Him to work through us to see that His will is done on this earth, just as it is in Heaven.

God inhabits, or comes alive, in us when we praise Him. God loves to be loved and adored. He loves for us to tell Him how truly great He is. Of course, we can't even begin to know how great He is unless we read and study The Bible.

Upon hearing that God desires praise, I've heard people comment, disgustedly, that He must be conceited or "really full of Himself." So, let's think about that. Who laid the foundations of the earth—in just six days![21] Who hung the stars in the sky? Who gives orders to the constellations and stars and calls them all by name? Who created the sun and moon to give light on the earth and to determine seasons? Who created the birds of the air, the beasts of the field and feeds the creatures of the deep? Who has a storehouse for snow and hail, thunder and lightning? Who sends the rain to bring forth fruit and vegetables in their season and who feeds and waters all of the creatures of the earth?[22] Who knit you carefully together in your mother's womb, wrote the number of your days in His book before you ever lived one of them and knows every word you are going to say before it ever leaves your tongue?[23] Who knows the number of hairs on your head?[24] Who chose you in Himself before the foundations of the earth were made?[25] Who

---

[19] Mt. 6:9,10
[20] Lev. 22:31,32; Gal. 3:29
[21] Gen. 1 & 2
[22] Job 38-40; Ps 147:4; Isa. 40:26
[23] Ps. 139
[24] Mt. 10:30; Lk. 12:7
[25] Jn. 15:16; Eph. 1:4

prayed for you in the Garden of Gethsemane?[26] Who knew you before you were ever born, called you by name and set you apart for His purpose?[27] Who has too many beautiful attributes to list them all? God, of course! Doesn't He have the right, then, to claim all glory and honor, majesty and praise from us, whom He created?

During your 'Prayer of Praise' it is good and appropriate to lift up your heart and voice in audible speech and song. Read the passages that detail things God has done and praise Him specifically for each one. You don't have to list everything all at once but each time, praise Him for something else—including the miracles you've seen in your own life and the lives of your spouse, children, grandchildren and others.

I like to read the Psalms and sing them to the Lord. It was during just such a time that The Lord gifted me with a heavenly language[28] with which to praise Him. I was surprised and listened to the cadence as it floated out onto the air. I think I stopped it because I became caught up in the event rather than praising my Lord. In retrospect, I believe it was similar to the experience of the Apostle Peter when Jesus allowed him to walk on the water.[29] He was proceeding along just fine until he took his eyes off of Jesus and began to look at his circumstances. When the realization hit that he was actually walking on water, he became terrified and lost all confidence. When you begin to praise The Lord, you and He will embark upon a special journey. Be sure to note in your journal the wonderful things that occur as you encounter God through your praises.

Pray Thanksgiving

Give us this day our daily bread.[30]

We are acknowledging that God is the Provider and Sustainer of all. He holds our very life in His omnipotent, compassionate hand.[31]

---

[26] Jn. 17:6ff
[27] Jer. 1:5; Jn. 10:3-5
[28] 1Cor. 14:2,4,.5
[29] Mt. 14:29-30
[30] Mt. 6:11
[31] Ac. 17:28

Thanksgiving is not the same as praise.

Thanksgiving is often purely an act of obedience[32] because God said, "Do it." It is not necessarily a feeling of thankfulness.[33] I will tell you, however, that as you determine to be obedient and give thanks, despite your feelings, God is faithful to bring a spirit of thanksgiving and joy. We give thanks for events God has allowed to occur in our lives. Sometimes thanksgiving comes easily: as, for instance, when there's money in the bank, food on the table, the children are doing well, people like us or we get a raise in pay. In those times, we are quick to give thanks. But what about those times when things aren't going so well? The prophet Habakkuk prayed it eloquently.[34] I will paraphrase his prayer in our modern vernacular:

> Though I'm out of work and have no money in the bank.
> Though no one is interested in hiring me
> and I have little or no food in my refrigerator,
> though my car is broken-down and I can't afford to fix it
> (if I did, I don't have gas money anyway).
> My friends turn away from me
> and I think they are laughing behind my back.
> My spouse says I have bad breath and my children shy away from me…
> But, I will still rejoice in The Lord!
> I will be joyful in God my Savior.
> Allison's Paraphrase

Once, when we owned an RV park, there was a week-long deluge of rain falling at an overwhelming rate! Our property was just 10-feet off the water table and we had 580,000 gallons of water pooled on the ground. To make matters worse, an underground water pipe broke due to shifting, sandy soil. Every time my husband and his maintenance workers tried to fix it, rain would pour! There were brine shrimp growing, bullfrogs croaking and water moccasins swimming. Folks had to use a boat or wade through this water to reach cars and homes. After three days of this, it again began to pour rain and my husband came into the house exhausted and discouraged. I suggested something that will probably sound really

---

[32] 1Th. 5:17; 1Sam.15:22Lp
[33] Job 1:20-22; Plp. 4:12-13
[34] Hbk. 3:17,18

crazy to you. I said, "Let's go sing praises to The Lord." We did! And while we were singing praises to Him, God impressed upon my husband exactly how to fix the problem—and it never happened again. We sang, not because we felt thankful; but because we know the Source of our help and we had reached the end of ourselves. God commands us, "in everything, and in every situation, give thanks."[35]

Does it help you to know that Satan can't bring adversity into our lives without first asking God for permission?[36] God doesn't always prevent Satan but He does limit him and Jesus always prays for us.[37] Can you imagine having such prayer support? Well, you do have it.

You might say, "…but only good gifts come from God." Actually, The Bible says "…every good gift and every perfect gift…"[38] In our human sight, we view circumstances through a warped lens. We see only the immediate affect—not the long term, eternal effect. As an example, we see sickness with its pain and devastation as a horrible thing—sometimes, we become angry with God. God sees the effect of His child's patience in suffering. He sees the eternal effect on others of His child's suffering, as they witness the circumstances and apparent faith. God loves us and He cares. He is moved with compassion when His children are hurting.[39]

God only allows trials in our lives that will work for our eternal good and His glory. You and I see the trial; God sees the beauty of the finished tapestry.

I know a woman who was always vibrantly healthy, strong and active. Suddenly, without warning, she was laid low, to the point of death, with catastrophic illness—not one but TWO systemic cancers! Doctors said she had two weeks to live and told her husband to get his affairs in order. This woman was so skinny! In a very short time, she lost over 70 pounds, could barely walk and couldn't eat. She was too sick to even pray. She simply told God, "I trust You with me." Did her husband get his material affairs in order? No. He said he was too busy getting people to pray for his wife.

---

[35] 1Th. 5:17 (repeat)
[36] Job 1:6-12; 2:3-6; Lk. 22:31-32
[37] Heb. 7:25Lp
[38] Jas. 1:17
[39] Ps. 40:11; 103:2-4; Lam. 3:22-23; 2 Cor. 1:3,4

The woman did not die. Recovery was slow; but God raised her from her sick bed and allowed her, once again, to speak and sing for Him. She and her husband and friends rejoiced in God and she thanked Jesus, with her whole heart, for entrusting her with suffering.[40]

Christian people will go through suffering. God promised it.[41] There is a devil loose on planet earth and he is full of fury because he knows his time is short.[42] He will do everything in his power to destroy Christians and Christian faith. We cannot expect to get accolades from society and the secular media—or many times even from our fellow Christians. Sometimes the very ones, from whom we expect to get validation, turn in hostility and malign rather than bless. God says, unless we stand in our faith, we won't stand at all.[43] Our victory is through our prayers of praise and thanksgiving and our confession of faith.[44] Notice, I said "our victory." I did not say "our salvation." I am talking here about our "victory" over Satan. Salvation comes only through Jesus' blood sacrifice (see section on Salvation). Our faith is built upon prayer and Bible study—one cannot successfully have one without the other.

Pray Confession and Repentance

Forgive us our trespasses as we forgive those who trespass against us.[45]

Here we are confessing our sins against God and one another. We are giving God permission to treat us the way we treat our fellow man. We are acknowledging that if we do not forgive others, God will not forgive us.

God tells us that we need to settle matters quickly with those with whom we have disputes[46] and He tells us how to do it.[47]

Jesus' teaching on **conflict resolution** is a four-step plan. Any confrontation should begin with much prayer about you, as well as the offender and the

---

[40] Author's personal reflection
[41] Jn. 16:33
[42] Rev. 12:12
[43] Isa. 7:9Lp
[44] 1Jn. 5:4,5
[45] Mt. 6:12,14,15
[46] Mt. 5:25
[47] Mt. 18:15-17

situation. The steps will be discontinued whenever the situation is resolved. Step 1. Go to the offender and in humility and with gentleness of spirit explain the problem, just between the two of you—do not tell anyone else. If your brother or sister listens, you have saved the relationship and there is no need to take the issue further. If, however, there is unwillingness to listen to you, move on to Step 2. Take one or two godly Christians with you in order to establish the issue in the presence of witnesses. If there is still a refusal to listen, move to step 3. Tell it to the church. This is usually the pastor or a Bible counselor designated to deal with such matters. (This is presupposing that you attend a Bible-based church that follows guidelines as set forth by Jesus.) If there is still a stubborn refusal to listen, even to the church then, as the last resort move on to 4. Sever ties of friendship or business but continue to treat the individual with the courtesy you would anyone you meet on the street. Continue to pray for the situation, asking God to bring repentance and forgiveness.

Mainstream preachers have stepped away from preaching repentance. The current thinking seems to be that people need to feel good about themselves and suggesting that they are sinners in need of repentance might prevent them from that good feeling. If they don't feel good about what they hear at church, they might not attend and consequently, won't give money. Unfortunately, in a great many churches, it's more about the financial bottom line than it is about conversion and repentance from sin.

When the apostles faithfully preached The Gospel of Jesus Christ and called for repentance, huge numbers were convicted by The Holy Spirit and joined the church.[48] Jesus called people to repent[49] and His disciples faithfully preached it.

Some Christians believe that once they receive Jesus as their Savior and join a church there is no further need to repent. The passage usually cited is the Apostle Paul speaking to Spirit-led men and women. These are people sincerely desiring and *practicing* the Christian walk but who still make mistakes. To those people the Apostle Paul says, "There is no condemnation to those who are in Christ Jesus."[50] Jesus didn't condemn

---

[48] Ac. 2:40Lp,41,47; 5:14
[49] Lk. 13:3Lp; 15:7 ; Ac. 26:20
[50] Rom. 8:1-2

the woman taken in adultery but she still needed to repent and be forgiven of her sins. Jesus indicates in His Revelation messages to the Churches[51] of Ephesus, Pergamum, Thyatira, Sardis and Laodicea that there is need for repentance in most of our lives. Each of the churches was commended for some good they were doing; but God said to them, "If you don't repent, I will pull your church out" by the roots. The message went to the pastor of the churches; but, both the pastor and the congregants were guilty of the sins for which they needed to repent. Jesus indicates that we should assess our Christian walk on an ongoing basis to see if it is faithful to Scripture. It's easy when listening to preachers to take whatever they say as if it came directly from The Word of God. Sadly, it often does not. The apostles commended the people they taught in Berea[52] because every day, after hearing the preaching, the people went home and "searched the Scriptures" to make sure that what they had been told was truth. **Do you do that?**

Do you check your pastor's preaching against The Word of God? You might be very surprised. God holds the pastor accountable for his or her teachings and holds them accountable for individuals they lead astray.[53] God holds each of us accountable for the choices we make—including the church teachings that we blindly accept.

Each of us should take a daily assessment of our Christian walk. God instructs us to pray in The Spirit on all occasions, confessing and repenting for sins of thought, word or deed, as The Holy Spirit makes us aware. We are to walk in The Spirit by talking to God, reading His Word and listening to His voice and then, of course, doing what He says. If we do this, there will be no need for anyone else to point out sins in our lives.

Pray Corporately

This is group prayer where two or more are involved.[54] Often we think of this as taking place in a formal setting but it can be very informal, as well. Married couples may choose to pray together kneeling by their bed or even in bed.

---

[51] Rev. 2:1ff; 3:1-22
[52] Ac. 17:11
[53] Jas. 3:1
[54] Mt. 18:19, 20

They may include honoring God by reading Scripture together in preparation for sleep. Corporate prayer may take place in someone's living room or in a basement prayer meeting, where participants take turns praying.

Churches often engage in corporate prayer. This may be in the form of liturgical prayers where the pastor or leader offers part of the prayer and then the congregation collectively joins in. Some churches refer to this as responsive reading. Corporate prayers are prayers of agreement where everyone is petitioning for a specific need.

A familiar prayer which is often prayed corporately is "The Lord's Prayer"[55] Prayers may be extemporaneous i.e., delivered spontaneously or may be prepared ahead of time and delivered without the use of notes. Prayers that are read often seem to lack sincerity. Corporate prayers are often banal, repetitive, unimaginative and boring.

God said He hates vain repetitions.[56] Prayers that are offered simply to fulfill the liturgy or so one can say they prayed or so the one praying may be seen and heard[57] is vain repetition.

Corporate prayers can be wonderful and God honors the prayer of agreement.[58] The problem that can occur is a banality, reading or reciting prayers without any real passion—simply going through the motions. The Lord's Prayer and liturgical prayers are often recited in this way. This kind of praying is a violation of the second commandment: Thou shalt not take The Lord's Name in vain or misuse His Name.[59]

Pray Privately

Lead us not into Temptation
but Deliver us from Evil[60]

---

[55] Mt. 6:9-13 KJV (NIV footnotes the last part of verse 13)
[56] Mt. 6:7 KJV
[57] Lk 18:10-14;
[58] Mt. 18:19,20; Ac. 2:1-4; Ps 133
[59] Ex. 20:7; Deut. 5:11
[60] Mt. 6:13

Private prayer refers to a time personally set apart for talking to God one-on-one, as one would to a friend. That old Satan will attempt to come up with every excuse to prevent you from keeping this appointment, but true victory and service comes out of this private communion time.

Jesus gave us the examples of going alone to pray, praying out loud and humility.

Jesus went away from the crowds and even away from His disciples, to a place where He was free to pour out His soul and His tears, as He sought strength and encouragement from The Father.[61]

Have you ever desired for God to use you to heal the sick, raise the dead, teach people in ways they cannot help but understand and to assist the Kingdom of God to come on earth, just as it is in Heaven? Well, you can do all of those things. God promised it;[62] but you have to be willing to invest in a similar prayer life.

We certainly can pray as we walk or drive, watch a sunset, shop and many other activities; but there is a special oneness with The Spirit of Jesus when we go to a quiet place alone to talk to God and listen for His answers. As a matter-of-fact, those to whom God entrusts great ministries, often seek and find time to be alone with Him. The great ministry to which God has entrusted you might be raising the children He has given you or loving your spouse; or perhaps some other task to which you haven't ascribed much priority.

Private prayers are usually in our common, every-day speech: friend-to-Friend. If we are able to kneel, as Jesus did, that is a wonderful gift and an act of humility before Our King. Many of us, however, because of health issues, are unable to kneel or even get out of bed or chair; but all of us can choose to be alone to converse with our Friend, Jesus. When you do converse with Jesus, pray out loud. There is power in the spoken prayer. There is power when your family hears their names spoken in prayer. In Jesus' private prayers, He prayed out loud. That's how His disciples were able to record His prayers. That's why they asked Jesus to teach them to

---

[61] Mt. 14:23; Mk. 6:46; Lk. 6:12; 22:39-44
[62] Mk. 16:15-18

pray. They heard His prayers and felt the power. They wanted that for themselves.

Imagine the effect on your children or spouse to hear you call their name in prayer. They will be strengthened in the face of temptation and social pressure. In John 17, Jesus' prayer prior to going to the cross is recorded. He prayed out loud and He called your name and mine.

I told you a friend once shared that she has her private prayer time in the bathroom. That's the only place she feels assured of being alone and uninterrupted. I will tell you that Jesus will meet you anywhere. He just wants you to spend time alone with Him—He is very jealous to spend time alone with you.

When I say Jesus is jealous, I don't mean He is jealous for Himself. He is jealous for *you* to receive the very best that you can from Him and to walk in His best blessings.

Jesus is our Friend who sticks closer than a brother, sister, mother or spouse. The Bible says that when everyone else forsakes you, The Lord will take you up.[63]

Pray Fasting

Before we discuss fasting and prayer, I would caution you not to enter into fasting lightly or in a spirit of jest. It is not a weight-loss plan and it is not a joke. I have heard individuals joke about Lenten fasts, saying they will give up a certain thing "because I don't like it anyway." Entering into a time of fasting before God is a serious matter and it is done when one desires a special encounter with Jesus (see One Triune God). He is always with us[64] and He hears every word we say.[65] This is a sober time of personal reflection to seek Jesus' Holy Spirit power.

---

[63] Ps. 27:10
[64] Mt. 28:20Lp
[65] Ps. 139:4

We need to take care that our fasting is not done as a means of drawing attention to ourselves. Jesus said, wash your face, comb your hair and be presentable so that it won't be obvious to others that you are fasting;[66] and do not announce what you are doing for God, so people will be impressed with you. In other words, put on your makeup, shave and wear clean clothes and do not preface every conversation with, "Uh, well…I'm fasting…" Just go quietly about this God-business and seek His strength and mighty power.

One day a man brought his son to the disciples for them to heal him from a sickness similar to epilepsy. They were unable to heal the boy. When Jesus came, He healed the young man. Afterward, He had a short class on "Faith" with His disciples. Jesus told them, "…this kind only come out by prayer and fasting."[67]

When Jesus fasted, He went without food—in one case for 40-days.[68] At another time He was traveling along with His disciples, ministering to the people, praying in The Spirit and fasting.[69]

Each of us needs to be directed by The Holy Spirit of Jesus as to how and what to fast. Some would not be able to fast all food for days at a time or even one day. Some might be directed by God to fast one meal. The Prophet Daniel fasted meat, fancy food and drink and limited himself to vegetables, fruits, nuts, legumes and water. This has come to be referred to as a "Daniel Fast."[70] Some choose to fast television or some other thing that they believe interferes with their time with God. What you fast is between you and Jesus. Each of us must be convinced in our own minds what God wants us to do. Do not, however, fast from reading God's Word or praying. That is never God's will. It is through The Bible and prayer that God speaks to us. Utilize every kind of prayer during your fast and keep notes as to how God leads you, as well as any changes that occur in your life.

---

[66] Mt. 6: 17,18
[67] Mt. 17:14-21-KJV (NIV footnotes this 21st verse)
[68] Mt. 4:2; Ac 14:23
[69] Jn. 4:31-34 (Jesus' food was the joy of finishing God's work)
[70] Daniel 9:3; 10:2,3

Pray Intercession

God is looking for men and women to stand in the gap before Him to make intercession for the nation, the church and the people.[71] Intercession is a special prayer that we pray for others when they need prayer support, when they cannot pray for themselves or even when they will not pray for themselves. Intercessors stand "in the gap" between earth and Heaven. God calls all believers to this type of prayer.

Biblical examples of intercessory prayer are found in stories of Abraham,[72] Moses,[73] Samuel,[74] an un-named man of God,[75] Job,[76] Jesus,[77] The Holy Spirit[78] and God's people.

God has commanded all of us to pray for the peace of Jerusalem[79] and He promises a blessing to those who bless her.

I told you the story of a woman so sick she couldn't pray for herself.[80] God surrounded her with many, many intercessors praying for her healing. God answered those prayers by raising her to health to encourage others and to tell what great things God has done.

God calls every Christian to intercessory prayer. Besides praying for Jerusalem, we are to pray for our leaders,[81] our enemies[82] and for one another.[83] God also calls certain individuals to a ministry of intercession.[84] Intercessors pray faithfully for those whom God has laid on their hearts throughout the church, the nation and the world. Sometimes God's call is specific to a family, a person or an event. It may be focused prayer for a

---

[71] Ezk. 22:30
[72] Gen. 18:16-33; 20:17
[73] Ex. 8:8-10, 28; Ps. 106:23
[74] 1Sam. 7:5
[75] 1Ki. 13:1, 6
[76] Job 42:8
[77] Isa. 53:12; Jn. 17; Rom. 8:34; 1Tim. 2:5,6; Heb. 7:25
[78] Rom. 8:26,27
[79] Ps. 122:6,7
[80] See personal reflection page 11; paragraph 4
[81] 1Tim. 2:1-3
[82] Lk. 6:28; Jas. 5:16; 1Jn 5:16; Jude 17-23
[83] Rom. 12:10-13; Gal. 6:2; Col. 3:13;Jas. 5:16
[84] Ezk.33:1-20

community, the country or the persecuted church. Perhaps you have been commissioned to pray for Our Lord's soon return for His saints.[85]

In each case, God's call is specific and it lies heavily on the heart of the one called. It is a task for which one feels unprepared, humbled and unworthy. Often it includes speaking messages to certain individuals or groups. When God calls the intercessor to speak, The Holy Spirit gives the words[86]—which may or may not be well received.

The Prophet Jeremiah had a ministry of intercession, which lay so heavily upon him that he was known as the "weeping prophet." He said he wished his head was a spring of water and his eyes a fountain to contain all of his tears.[87] The ministry of intercession is not glamourous.

A true intercessor's prayers are directed by God and may include fasting. God will give the intercessor spiritual insight into situations in order to direct their prayers. This God-given insight is not for gossip and may only be disclosed by God's direction.

Pray Jesus' Name

God has prescribed a way for us to pray to Him and that way is through The Name of Jesus.[88]

You might wonder why we can't just pray to "God." First of all, Satan sets himself up as god and the name god is used to describe many entities, including Ishtar, the goddess of fertility, a Babylonian god also known as Ashtoreth[89] and as Queen of Heaven; Molek,[90] the detestable god of the ancient Sidonians to whom children were sacrificed in the fire; Allah,[91] the god of Islam, previously known as the moon god, who requires jihad,

---

[85] 1Th. 4:16-18
[86] Lk.12:11,12; Jn. 14:26
[87] Jer. 9:1
[88] Jn. 14:13,14; 15:6,7; 16:23-28; Ac. 4:11,12
[89] 1Ki.11:5; 2Ki,23:13ff
[90] Lev 20:2-5
[91] Arab new mythology; Wikipedia; Quran chapter 41; v37

intifada and participant suicide. There are many other gods. The worship of these entities by God's children provoked Him to anger.[92]

The Name "Jesus" describes but ONE God: God Almighty, Maker of Heaven and Earth.

When God chose to become like His children and take on flesh and blood[93] in order to die for our sins, He made a way for us to go to Heaven. The prescribed way is to present our requests and pray for our needs in Jesus' Name; thus acknowledging our acceptance of His sacrificial gift. That is why He told His disciples: "I will do whatever you ask in My Name." The Name "Jesus" is God's Name that unlocks Heaven's door.[94] Jesus' Name brings answers and Heaven's bounty. When you go to your safety deposit box, get into your car or enter your house, there is only ONE key that operates the lock. The Name of Jesus is the ONE specific key that opens to us Heaven's door.

Some close their prayers with, "in Your Name" or "in Your Son's Name," etc. With these vague, lackluster sign-offs, your prayers will lack Holy Spirit power. Do not hesitate to pray in Jesus' Name. Do not be ashamed to use Jesus' Name. JESUS is your golden key to victory!

Many of you may have grown up praying to Mary or saints canonized by a church. Nowhere in Scripture does God give us permission to use any name in our prayers but The Name of Jesus. Some might ask, "Well, didn't the servants at the wedding feast in Cana[95] go to Jesus' mother to ask her to intercede with her Son to get them wine?" No, they did not. Mary took it upon herself, when she saw that they had run out of wine, to go to Jesus[96] and tell Him of the predicament. His response, "Woman, why are you bothering me with this...?" Mary turned to the servants and said, "Do whatever He says." Just like any proud mother, she wanted everyone to know her son's capabilities. As a respectful son, and so as not to embarrass her, Jesus fulfilled her request.

---

[92] Jer. 7:18; 44:16-25ff
[93] Heb. 2:14.17
[94] Jn. 14:13;15:16; Ac. 4:12;18-20;16:25,26
[95] Jn. 2:1,2
[96] Jn. 2:3

Others will say that they don't pray to ask Mary or the saints to intercede with God. They go to Mary and the saints to intercede with Jesus and He in turn goes to God. If you have completed the study on "One Triune God." you will understand without a shadow of a doubt that Jesus IS God. He is God Almighty, He is God the Creator. He is the One God. Aside from Him, there is no other[97] (see One Triune God).

There are only a few times that Jesus' mother is mentioned in Scripture. The first time, of course, is at His birth. The second time was when she and His brothers went looking for Him[98] in a house where He was teaching. Their plan was to "take charge of Him" because they thought He was out of His mind. The last time we hear specifically of Jesus' mother is at the cross when Jesus gave her into the care of His best earthly friend and disciple, John.[99]

Final Thoughts on Prayer

The Bible says that, in Heaven, angels hold golden bowls full of incense. This incense is the prayers of the saints[100] going up before God as a sweet aroma. Prayer in all forms is a wonderful way to take hold of the power of Jesus Christ by His Spirit. Jesus obtained His strength through prayer and many times combined prayer with fasting. The Bible says that Jesus' activities are the activities of God. He never did anything apart from God's activity. What a difference God's people would make in this world if our prayer lives opened us to God's voice and direction. What a difference then, if we never did anything that we were not told by The Holy Spirit to do. We can tap into that power. Jesus told us that we will do all the things He did while He was here, and even more![101] I believe, if we truly knew the power available to us, we would run to talk to Jesus. Satan understands the power available to Christians and he will do all he can to prevent us from taking advantage of it by spending time with Jesus.

Prayer unanswered: God loves to answer our prayers. If you have read and studied through this section on prayer, you know that sometimes, even

---

[97] Isa. 45:18-22; Ac. 4:12; Jude 24,25
[98] Mk. 3:21,31-35
[99] Jn. 19:26,27
[100] Rev. 5:8Lp
[101] Jn. 14:12

though we are praying fervently, we may not be praying according to God's will.[102] In those cases, The Holy Spirit comes along side and prays the prayer for us and intercedes on our behalf.[103] We also learned that sometimes, even when we are praying correctly, the answer may be intercepted by unholy angels.[104] Sometimes God's answer is for us to wait, because the timing is not right; in that case God tells us to keep on praying and don't give up[105] God will give us the answer in His time.

In Mark 16, God outlined things that the believing Christian will have power to do.[106] He says when those who put their faith in Him, pick up snakes with our hands or drink "deadly poison," it won't hurt them at all. This is not an invitation to indulge in presumptuous sin. There are groups that actually make handling snakes part of their religious ritual. God is not suggesting that. His Word is simply saying that when wicked people verbally or physically tear us apart God will protect us. Throughout Scripture, snakes denote satanic activity. When confrontation with "snakes" and "poisons" are inevitable, God will protect us and give us His peace that passes earthly understanding.[107] My husband and I claimed this promise in Mark 16 when massive doses of IV chemotherapy were necessary for cancer treatment. We prayed that God would assist the medicine to do only good and not harm.

We do not willingly encounter negative things but when we are forced into such situations, we trust God and He delivers us.[108] What I'm saying here is, in so far as it depends upon us, Christians must choose to live at peace with everyone.[109] We sometimes think we are so holy that we are justified in being unkind to neighbors and strangers or speaking rudely. God would not have us look down on those who don't believe as we do. Tattoos and piercings are not our cue to find fault and look down on anyone.[110] Someone may worship on a day different than us, or eat or drink things we don't.[111] God wants us to ask Him to help us see the heart of the

---

[102] Jas. 4:3
[103] Rom. 8:26
[104] Dan. 10:12,13
[105] Lk. 18:1-8
[106] Mk. 16:17-18
[107] Php. 4:7
[108] Ac. 28:2-6
[109] Rom.12:18; Php.4:8,9
[110] 1Sam. 16:7
[111] Rom. 14

individual, as He does, and treat each person with dignity and respect. If we are mistreated because we are miserable people, we deserve it. But when we are true ambassadors of Jesus Christ, loving and respectful and are still mistreated,[112] God promises to care for us, both here and in eternity.

Teach me to pray, Lord, teach me to pray
This is my heart cry day unto day;
I long to know Thy will and Thy way
Teach me to pray, Lord. teach me to pray.

Living in thee, Lord, and Thou in me.
Constant abiding, this is my plea.
Grant me Thy power, boundless and free;
Power with men and power with Thee.[113]

---

[112] Mt. 5:10-12; 2Tim.3:12
[113] Teach Me To Pray; Albert Simpson Reita; 1879-1966

Prayer Revisited

1. Did you take time to check out the study texts?
   All ___ Some ___ None___

2. Do you wear God's Armor? (Eph. 6:10ff) Yes___ No___

3. Do you find it easy to Praise God? Yes___ No___

4. Do you find yourself praying, praising and thanking God throughout your day? Yes___ No___

5. Can you think of a time when you thanked God when you really didn't feel like it? Yes___ No___ If "yes", what happened?_____
   _____

6. Have you felt the need to confess sins and repent? Yes____ No___

7. Is fasting part of your prayer life? Yes___ No___

8. Do you think fasting will become part of your prayer Life? Yes___ No___

9. Has God ever used you to intercede in prayer for someone else? Yes___ No___

   When? _____

10. How would you like to see your prayer life change? _____
    _____

11. Do you regularly set aside a quiet time to be alone with God? Yes___ No___

12. Do you pray out loud? Yes___ No___

13. Have you felt God tugging at you, calling you to spend time alone with Him? If yes, how did you respond? _____

14. Have you ever felt God speak to you? Yes__ No___I'm not sure __

15. Name a place where you could be alone with Jesus _____

16. Do you always pray in the Name of Jesus? Yes_____ No___

17. Do you believe praying in Jesus' Name is important? Yes___ No___

18. Are you troubled when pastors and leaders say, "…we pray this in Your Name" or "…we pray this in Your Son's Name" instead of speaking The Name of Jesus? Yes.___ No___

19. If yes, do you believe God would have you speak out about this? Yes___ No___

The Church

Jesus built His church upon Himself, the Spiritual Rock[1] who accompanied His children on their journey through the desert from Egypt and still accompanies His children today. Certainly, He did not build His church upon the Apostle Peter, as certain churches are prone to teach. Peter was an important disciple and apostle in the ministry of The Gospel; but he was also a very fallible human being. Shortly after Jesus proclaimed that He was building His church upon "this Rock," Jesus said to Peter, "Get behind Me, Satan! You are a stumbling block to me; you do not have in mind the things of God..."[2] Churches seem to take whatever conveniently fits their particular doctrine, without care to preaching the truth. That's why Jesus warned us to "beware of false prophets" who come in sheep's clothing but inside they are ravening wolves.[3]

Jesus appointed His church to be the vessel to proclaim The Gospel around the world. It began in Jerusalem; and spread through persecution and martyrdom. The blood of martyrs has seeded the church of Jesus Christ throughout history. The persecution of the church has always been perpetrated first by leaders in the established church and then by despotic leaders around the world.

Martyrs whose stories are told in the Book of Acts are James the son of Zebedee, who was killed by the sword[4] and Stephen who was stoned to death.[5] The Jewish historian, Josephus, records that James, the brother of Jesus, was stoned to death.[6] According to early church tradition, the Apostle Peter was crucified at Rome and requested to be hung up-side-down because he thought himself unworthy to be crucified in the same manner as His Lord Jesus. The second century historian Tertullian reports that the Apostle Paul was beheaded in Rome and John was plunged into a cauldron of boiling oil, from which God rescued him, unhurt.[7] Afterward, John was exiled to the Isle of Patmos, where he was given The Revelation

---

[1] 1Cor. 10:4
[2] Mt. 16:23
[3] Mt. 10:15,16; Ac. 20:29-31
[4] Ac. 12:1,2
[5] Ac. 7:59
[6] Antiquities of the Jews; Josephus
[7] Prescription Against Heretics, Chapter 36; Dan. 3:19-27

of Jesus Christ. Most of the apostles were martyred. Would you give up your life to support a lie? The apostles truthfully proclaimed what they had actually witnessed and then willingly gave their lives to defend it.

I think of the second-century martyr from Smyrna, Turkey in Asia Minor. His name was Polycarpus (Polycarp). He was eighty-six when he was burned at the stake for his devotion to Jesus Christ. Persecutors tried to persuade him to recant his faith by coaxing that he was too old to die in this way. He responded, "Eighty-six years I have served Christ and He has never done me any harm. How, then, could I blaspheme my King who saved me? ...I bless Thee (God) for deigning me worthy of this day and this hour, that I may be among Thy martyrs and drink the cup of my Lord Jesus Christ."[8]

Polycarp was a convert of the disciple John, who subsequently wrote the Book of Revelation. Polycarp was the bishop of the church in Smyrna, the second church in Revelation to receive a letter from Jesus. Christians in Smyrna were being tortured and murdered and at eighty-six years old, he learned that there was a cry for his death. He escaped and went into hiding, but a young child found his hiding place. Polycarp had opportunity to escape again; but, in a dream, he had seen his bed in flames and believed God was letting him know that he would be martyred in this way. When soldiers appeared to arrest him, he first fed them and then requested time to pray. His request was granted. History records that Polycarp prayed fervently for one hour, during which time, his arrest detail wished they had not come for him. Once his prayer was finished, he calmly, serenely and with a cheerful demeanor allowed himself to be taken to the marketplace. He continued to pray fervently as his hands were bound and he was led to the stake. As the fire burned, Polycarp sang praises to God and the flames could not kill him. Witnesses said the smell was that of bread baking. The solders began throwing spears at him and history reports that the flow of his blood put out the flames. Finally, after many attempts, they managed to kill him. Afterward, they burned the body they could not burn in life.[9]

Today, Christians around the world are still paying with their lives for their devotion to Jesus Christ.

---

[8] Foxes Christian Martyrs of the World; Moody Press 187_; Christian History Institute
[9] FCM (footnote bottom of previous page); pages 55, 56

And I heard a voice from Heaven saying to me,
"Write, 'Blessed are the dead which die in The Lord from now on.'
"Yes," says The Spirit,
"They will rest from their labors;
"For their works will follow them."[10]

God has allowed the suffering of His saints to promote and further The Gospel. Some, who witnessed the horrors of these martyrs' fate, gave their lives to Jesus Christ, thereby gaining for themselves eternal life.

It will be worth it all, when we see Jesus.
Life's trials will seem so small
when we see Christ.
One glimpse of His dear face,
all sorrows will erase.
So, bravely run the race,
'til we see Christ.[11]

God has singled out the church as His precious bride. John the Baptist first used that term for Jesus' followers when his own disciples complained to him that all the people were leaving John's ministry and going over to Jesus. John said, "I am not The Christ, I am sent ahead of Him. The bride belongs to The Bridegroom and those who follow Him listen and are filled with joy when they hear The Bridegroom's voice. That joy is mine and it is now complete."[12]

In the parable of the five wise and five foolish virgins, Jesus told a story about guests waiting for The Bridegroom.[13] Jesus frequently referred to Himself as The Bridegroom and said the time would come when He would be taken from them. He went on to tell them to watch, because we do not know the day or the hour when He will return.[14] We are admonished to be wise and be doing what Jesus has put before us to do when He gets here, even if the wait seems like a long time.[15]

---

[10] Rev. 14:13
[11] Esther Kerr Rusthoi, 1909-1962; copy write ASCAP 1941
[12] Jn. 3:29
[13] Mt. 25:1-13
[14] Mt. 25:13
[15] Mt.. 24:46; Lk. 12:37,38,43

Jesus tells us He will come for a bride (the church) who has made herself ready.[16] She will be clothed in fine linen (the righteous acts of the saints).[17]

> Blessed are those who are invited
> to the Wedding Supper of The Lamb.[18]

It is up to us to work out our salvation with fear and trembling.[19] It is up to us to see that we are hearing truth from our pulpits. God has told us, through His Word, to guard against those who do not teach sound doctrine.[20] There are a lot of churches who adhere more and more closely to the social programs of the world than to the truth of The Bible. God warned that the time would come when men will not put up with truth but instead will gather teachers who will tell them whatever their itching ears want to hear.[21]

Unfortunately, most of us do not know The Bible well enough to know a falsehood if it hit us in the face and Satan takes advantage of our ignorance. The Bible says Satan masquerades as an angel of light and that he has preachers and teachers in our pulpits who, likewise, masquerade as angels of light.[22] We accept these charlatans without question; but, sadly, they are teaching doctrines from hell.[23]

It's easy when listening to preachers to take whatever they say as if it came directly from The Word of God. Sadly, it often does not. The apostles commended the people they taught in Berea[24] because every day, after hearing the apostles preach, the people went home and "searched the Scriptures" to make sure that what they had been told was truth. **Do you do that?**

Do you check your pastor's preaching against the Word of God? Sometimes the message can be so scrambled that you are unsure what really was

---

[16] Eph. 5:25-27; Php. 2:12; Rev. 19:7-8
[17] Ibid. v. 8
[18] Ibid. v. 9
[19] Php. 2:12Lp
[20] 2Tim. 1:12,14; Prov. 4:13,23
[21] 2Tim. 4:3,4
[22] 2 Pet. 2:1-3,9; 2Cor. 11:13-15
[23] Mt. 23:15
[24] Ac. 17:11

taught. When you can decipher it, you might be very surprised to know that it doesn't match up to God's Word. God holds the pastor accountable for his or her teachings and holds the teacher accountable for individuals who are led astray.[25] God expects us to know His Word well enough to be able to discern between holy and unholy spirits and to rightly divide the Word of Truth.[26]

Final Thoughts on the Church

Someone once said the church is a hospital for sinners; not a museum for saints. This is a catchy little platitude but we need not be overly proud of ourselves for either our sinful or saintly aspects. Both positions, taken to extreme will be our undoing. Instead, we need to pull together to encourage and lift up one another. When God told us not to forsake going to church[27] it was so that each of us may be an encouragement to someone else.

> How good and pleasant it is
> When brothers and sisters
> come together in unity!
> It is like precious oil poured on the head,
> It is as refreshing as the dew of
> Mount Herman falling on Mount Zion.
> There the Lord bestows His blessings,
> even life forevermore. [28]

---

[25] Jas. 3:1
[26] 2Tim. 2:15
[27] Heb. 10:25
[28] Ps. 133

Church Revisited

1. Did you take time to check out the study texts?
    All ____ Some ____ None____

2. Who is The Rock on whom Christ built His church? (1Cor. 10:4)

    _____

3. How did The Gospel of Jesus Christ spread around the world?

    _____

4. How did martyrs, such as the disciples and Polycarp find the strength to die for Christ? (Php.4:13)_____

5. Are you looking forward to participating in The Wedding Supper of The Lamb? Yes.____ No____

6. Do you set aside time, daily, to read and study The Bible?
    Yes____ No____

    Do you know if your Pastor is preaching truthfully from The Bible?
    Yes____ No____ Unsure____

7. Do you pray for your pastor? Yes____ No____ Sometimes____

8. How do you encourage your pastor to preach truth from God's Word?_____

    _____

PROSPERITY GOSPEL
Word of Faith
...which, really, is no gospel at all[1]

In the last fifty years or so, a new gospel has entered our churches. Ungodly preachers have taken over many pulpits—at first surreptitiously but then more and more boldly. They have begun to tell stories and preach heresies they have made up.[2] They claim to have new revelation from God on how to get wealth and how to prosper. They pander to our human desires to acquire wealth, material goods and keep up with the Joneses.

First, Psalm 37:4 is misquoted, proclaiming that God wants to give you the desires of your heart. Actually the verse says, "Delight yourself in The Lord and He will give you the desires of your heart." Might it be that as we delight in The Lord, the desires of our hearts will change from desires of self-gratification to what God truly desires for us? God desires that we do His will and assist His will to be done on this earth, just as it is in Heaven.

The message usually mixes some truth with a lot of effort; but if you don't know Scripture, you won't know that. Usually, the prosperity preacher's message is that we do not have because we do not give enough—this is referred to as "sowing seed." The reference is always to money. The message is, "Give out of your need." In other words, if you are so needy that you cannot make it to the next payday, give out of that need. Often, a suggestion will be made as to an amount for you to give: $100, $1000 and so on. They will tell you to give and it will be given back to you, good measure pressed down and running over will be poured into your bosom."[3]

God did tell us to give to God and to others and with the measure we use in our giving, it will be given back to us; but there are more ways to give to Kingdom-work than simply giving money. The giving God desires from you could be to care for your family or someone in need, as in the story of the Good Samaritan.[4] Using your God-given talents of hospitality, teaching, building, singing, etc., to bless others and looking after orphans

---

[1] Gal. 1:6-9
[2] 2Pet. 2:3
[3] Lk. 6:38
[4] Lk. 10:30-36

and widows[5] will bring glory to The Lord and are legitimate ways in which we give to The Kingdom.[6]

The prosperity gospel majors on money. The more money one gives, per this philosophy, the more one will receive. Some preachers will actually say that if you give $100 you will reap ten-fold: $1000. If you sow $1000, you will reap $10,000…and so on. Sometimes the return is ratcheted up to 100-fold. It's like God is the great slot-machine in the sky!

This "name-it-and-claim-it" mentality spills over into everything; but health issues are a special focus. In that case, it is combined with "Word of Faith" and the teaching is to demand healing. Never pray for God's will to be done since, they say, it is always God's will to heal (see Healing). Never tell anyone you are sick, do not admit it and do not talk about it because this is negative speech. God will not heal you if you speak negative words. Definitely, never let on to anyone that you are facing death since talking about it might make it happen. Just speak positive things to yourself and about yourself. This is a takeoff on "mind-over-matter." There is a text for every situation; no matter that it may be taken out of context.

In the first place, it is God who told us to bear one another's burdens.[7] How can we carry one another's burdens if we never let anyone know we have any? God's people, whose lives are recorded in Scripture, always talked with their families about impending death. They would say, "I am about to go the way of all the earth…"[8] and then they would speak blessings or, in some cases, curses over their family. They would make requests of them, too and speak encouraging words to them. It might interest you to know that the words spoken over their families actually came to be. Perhaps knowing that will help us weigh more carefully the words we pronounce over our spouses and children.

We are never to demand anything from God;[9] we are to humbly make requests and seek His will. We can safely trust Him to do right.[10]

---

[5] Jas. 1:27
[6] Mic. 6:8
[7] Gal. 6:2
[8] Gen. 49:29-33; Josh. 23:14
[9] Isa. 45:11; Rom. 9:20,21
[10] Gen. 18:25Lp

A huge problem with the prosperity philosophy—besides being a dishonest portrayal of The Gospel of Jesus—is that it panders to our vanity and greed. The faith that it encourages is faith in material wealth and one's own ability to acquire it and bring about various events. Participants may become involved in shady financial schemes believing God will use these schemes to bring them wealth. They may depend upon doctrines of denial to bring them health. Since there is no real Bible truth on which to grow faith in Jesus Christ, participants often become discouraged and fall away from Christ when dreams do not materialize.[11]

I attended an Easter service at a church in Ohio. A prosperity preacher was the speaker on that Easter morning. In the sanctuary, which held a few thousand, there was standing room only. The preacher spent the entire service telling how he gave money to various other prosperity ministries and, miraculously, people chose to buy him thousand-dollar suits, expensive ties and cars. His house, which he said was paid for and very grand, sat on a park-like estate. He said people would rather go to his grand house than to a resort…and on and on and on. Not ONE word did he speak about Jesus dying for anyone's sins. Not ONE word did he speak about Jesus' resurrection from the dead—and this was EASTER, the one weekend out of the whole year when more people attend Christian services than any other! He took up several offerings and in one offering actually encouraged people to put in their wedding rings and other jewelry—some did! He truly fleeced the flock!

Fleecing the flock was also a function of religious leaders during Jesus' days here on earth. Devout followers of God were forced to purchase, at exorbitant prices, doves or lambs for their temple sacrifices. These had to be purchased at the temple using the temple shekel. The prosperity gospel is just another variation of that.

In the first century, Jesus went through the temple courts and threw the ill-gotten gains on the floor. He drove the money changers from the temple and proclaimed, "My Father's house shall be called a House of Prayer for all nations; but you have made it a den of thieves!"[12]

---

[11] 1Tim. 6:8-16
[12] Mt. 21:13; Mk 11:17; Lk. 19:46

God does not want His people to be demeaned, oppressed or fleeced by the very leaders to whom they look for encouragement and positive growth.

Final Thoughts on Prosperity Gospel

Hebrews chapter eleven is otherwise known as "The Faith Chapter."[13] God has listed many, but not all, of the godly people whose stories are told in the Old Testament. He tells how these Christians were persecuted, stoned, sawn in half, burned in the fire, forced to live in holes and caves and go about destitute in sheepskin, goatskin and rags. Like the martyrs of the first century and martyrs today, this world was not, and is not, worthy of them

Now, does this sound to you like these people lived in prosperity? Certainly, not by this world's standards. All of these people have their eyes set on a city without foundations who's Builder and Maker is God. If they were looking for the wealth of this world they could have renounced their faith and returned to a more comfortable lifestyle. What these saints did receive was God's miraculous provision, His miraculous faith, His miraculous strength. Some received loved ones back from the dead but they all received, for their faith, the commendation of God.

God has given us His formula for prosperity:

Seek ye first the Kingdom of God
And all of these other things will be given to you, as well.[14]

You see, when we seek first God's kingdom, He knows He can trust us with His provision.[15]

---

[13] Heb.11
[14] Mt. 6:33
[15] Deut. 28:1-14; Hag.1:3-11; Mal. 3:8-12

Prosperity Revisited

1. Did you take time to check out the study texts?
   All ___ Some ___ None___

2. Do you delight yourself in The Lord? Sing, pray, & dance before Him? Yes___ No___ I will ___

3. Do you ask God to help you bear, in prayer, the burdens of others? Yes___ No___

4. Has anyone faithfully prayed and shared your burdens? Yes___ No___

5. Do you regularly attend church in order to encourage fellow Christians? Yes___ No___

6. Did you take time to read the eleventh chapter of Hebrews? Yes___ No ___

   (Be sure to read, also, the first verse in chapter 12)

GIFTS OF THE SPIRIT[1]
Wisdom, Knowledge, Faith,
Gifts of Healing, Miraculous Powers, Prophecy,
Ability to distinguish between Spirits,
Speaking in Different Kinds of Tongues.
Apostles, Prophets, Teachers, Helps, Administration
The Holy Spirit distributes them, as He determines.

Wisdom is God. Wisdom comes from God. Wisdom is given to us when we ask God for it and when we read, understand and speak God's Word.

Knowledge is God's gift to help us understand His Word, clear up murky situations, and shine His light on uncertain circumstances. Words of knowledge may be for delivery to an individual or a group.

Faith is trust and confidence in God. In Scripture, we find that Stephan was a Christian described as full of The Holy Spirit and full of faith.[2] The disciples were described, in their growth phase, as having little faith.[3] Jesus said that if our faith in Him is as tiny as a grain of mustard seed[4] we can do exploits (that means to make full use of the God-resource we have in Jesus Christ). Our faith grows as we exercise it—as we step into the water and witness God's faithfulness.[5] When we enter upon tough times and choose to stand in belief that God will resolve the situation—and then we see Him do it! Our faith grows.

Gifts of Healing[6] come from God to show forth His glory and to attract the attention of others to His mighty works. Many times one through whom God chooses to manifest healing has, themselves, been miraculously healed; but more importantly, they have prayed and sought this ministry gift.

Speaking in Different kinds of Tongues[7] is varied. In Acts 2, Christ's followers were speaking in their own language; but, they were being heard

---

[1] 1Cor. 12:7-11, 28
[2] Ac. 6:5
[3] Mk. 16:14
[4] Mt. 17:20; Lk. 17:6
[5] Josh. 3:13
[6] Ac. 5:14,15
[7] Ac. 2:3

in the languages of their hearers. God has given gifts to individuals to be fluent in tongues other than their native language and this indeed is a blessing. But the spiritual gift of tongues can also be speaking or understanding language never before spoken. Gifts of tongues may occur when God wants to use an individual to share The Gospel in extenuating circumstances—as occurred in Acts 2. God also gifts individuals with a special prayer language. This is a language specifically used in prayer and praise to God.[8] This language is musical in its cadence and rise and fall. The one speaking may not know what is being said; but they will understand that they are praising and glorifying God. The Apostle Paul counsels that the one to whom God has given this language should pray that God will also give the interpretation. He also said, "I speak in tongues more than any of you and I wish you all did speak in tongues; but I would rather that you spoke understandable words to uplift and encourage one another.[9]

Scripture also tells us that tongues, when spoken in a group, should be used in an orderly manner with one person speaking at a time. Unless there is someone present who can interpret the message, tongues should not be spoken at all.

We should all earnestly desire all of these spiritual gifts and pray for them. As a note of caution, if The Holy Spirit wants you to speak in tongues He is very capable to make it happen. It is not necessary to go to someone who offers to teach you how to speak in tongues and says, "Repeat after me...." No, No, No. Just as there are genuine, spiritual gifts, the great deceiver can manifest counterfeit gifts.[10] The Holy Spirit gives these spiritual gifts to anyone He chooses. Do not attempt to manufacture this gift.

Some groups believe that anyone who does not speak in tongues does not have The Holy Spirit. The congregants often go about attempting to "practice tongues." God says The Spirit gives these gifts to whomever He determines—so there is no need to stress over it. Also The Bible says that unless The Spirit draws us we will not be interested in the things of God. God-things will appear to be foolishness to people without the Holy

---

[8] See Pray Praise page 9 last paragraph
[9] 1Cor 14: 18,19
[10] Mt. 24:24; Eph. 5:6

Spirit.[11] God tells us that He deposits His spirit in us as a guarantee of what is to come.[12] So, the new convert to Christianity immediately has The Holy Spirit within. The Spirit within him or her grows to fullness through study, prayer and obedience to God's will.

Apostle or **Evangelist** is a **Disciple** of Jesus Christ who is sent out as an envoy or ambassador of Jesus Christ to spread The Gospel message.

Prophet is one gifted in explaining prophetic utterances from the past and their relationship apocalyptically.

Teachers or **Pastors** explain The Gospel and biblical truths to various-sized groups.

Helps are used usually by laypeople to assist in the work of the ministry in any way needed.

Administration gifts are to assist God's work to be organized and flow smoothly.

---

[11] 1Cor. 1:18,23; 2:14
[12] 2Cor. 5:5; Eph. 1:13,14

Spiritual Gifts Revisited

1. Did you take time to check out the study texts?
   All ___ Some ___ None___

2. After reading this section, have you identified some areas in which The Holy Spirit has gifted you? Yes___ No___

3. What gifts did The Holy Spirit give you? _____

4. Will you, or do you now, use your gifts in the church?
   Yes ___ No___

5. Are you able to look around your church or Christian group and identify individuals with various gifts? Yes ___ No___

6. Has The Holy Spirit ever allowed you to speak in tongues?
   Yes___ No___

7. Do you pray for ALL of the spiritual gifts? Yes___ No___

8. If not ALL, for which ones will you pray?_____

9. Did you enjoy reading about Spiritual Gifts?_____

God first instituted the tithe with Abraham (Abram) in about 2000 B.C., long before the Levitical priesthood. God called Abraham to leave the land of his youth and go into a land that He would show him. I love the fact that Abraham obeyed and went, not knowing where he was going.[1]

Abraham took his wife, Sarah (Sarai) and his nephew, Lot and set out. Both Abraham and Lot had flocks and herds and The Bible records that after a time, Lot's herdsmen and Abraham's herdsmen quarreled because there wasn't enough land for all the flocks and herds to graze and get water. So Abraham and Lot decided to separate from each other. Abraham gave Lot first pick of the land and Lot chose the beautiful, lush land of Sodom.

Sometime after they separated, five kings, including the kings of Sodom and Gomorrah, banded together for battle against four enemy kings. The five kings, who included Sodom and Gomorrah, fled and the four kings captured everything in Sodom, including Lot, his family and all of his herds. Someone, who had escaped, hurried to tell Abraham of Lot's plight.[2]

Abraham mustered the three-hundred and eighteen trained fighting men who were born into his family. They rescued Lot and all of his possessions, along with all the people who had been captured.

Upon Abraham's return, he was met by Melchizedek, King of Salem. This king brought with him bread and wine (a precursor of the Passover, perhaps?) Melchizedek blessed Abraham by God Most High, Creator of heaven and earth. He said,

> "Blessed be God Most High
> who delivered your enemies into your hand."[3]
> Abraham gave Melchizedek a tenth of everything.

Jesus is our great High priest who has gone through the heavens. Jesus did not take the high priest role upon Himself. Prior to stepping out of Majesty

---

[1] Heb. 11:8
[2] Gen. 14
[3] Gen. 14:18-20

to become the Son of God, it was spoken of Jesus, "Thou art my Son, today I have begotten thee." In another place it was said, Thou art a priest forever in the order of Melchizedek...The Lord has spoken and will not change His mind. You are a priest forever.[4]

Melchizedek was King of Salem and Priest of God Most High. He met Abraham returning from war and Abraham gave him a tenth of everything. First, Melchizedek's name means "King of Righteousness;" then "King of Salem" which means "King of Peace."[5] Without father or mother, without genealogy, without beginning of days or end of life, like the Son of God, He remains a priest forever.

In the Book of Malachi, God indicted His people for robbing Him. They responded, "When did we ever rob You?"

God told them, "You've robbed Me in tithes and offerings. Every one of you is under a curse because you have robbed Me." He continued

> Bring all of the tithe into the storehouse
> So that there can be food in my house.
> Test Me in this.
> See if I don't open the windows of Heaven
> And pour out for you a blessing
> you will not have room enough to receive.[6]

God promises to bless us when we get up, when we lie down. We will be blessed in the city and blessed in the country. Our cupboards will be full, our children will be blessed. God will open the storehouses of Heaven and abundantly bless the work of our hands. He promises that enemies who come at us from one direction will flee from us in seven.[7]

Some will say that since this text is found in The Old Testament, it doesn't apply to New Testament Christians. First of all, there is no such thing as a Christian that lives only by the New Testament. One cannot worship a God

---

[4] Heb. 7:21
[5] Heb. 7:1ff
[6] Mal. 3:6-17
[7] Deuteronomy 28:1ff

one doesn't know and, if you don't read and believe The Old Testament, you don't know God. Jesus is The God of The Old Testament. He told the religious leaders, "If you believed Moses you would believe Me; because Moses testified about Me. All of the stories of the greatness, compassion and gifts of God in The Old Testament are stories of the pre-incarnate Christ. When you know The Old Testament, you know and understand the faithfulness of God. He never failed to follow through on what He promised. He is a covenant-keeping God. If you have never read the Old Testament, I challenge you to read it now.

Secondly, Malachi is a book about the Second Coming of Christ.

Third, if you think you are exempt from tithes and offerings because you are not an Israelite, you need to think again. God's Word declares, "If you are Christ's you are Abraham's seed and heirs according to the promise."[8]

When my good friend was confronted with tithing, he had a lot of reasons why it wasn't convenient to give that much. Finally, he said, "Okay, I'll try it for three months; but I really don't see how it can be done." So, he began tithing on net income. At the end of three months he told me, in amazement, "I don't know how I'm doing it, but I am! So, now I guess I'll keep on." Not long after that, he announced that he was going to begin tithing on gross income. Very soon, everything began to fall apart.[9] He had a piece of property with a dock on it that he had put up for sale for a fair price. People looked at it, but no one bought it. Then a huge storm came through and broke up the dock. He was very distressed when he told me about it. "So," I said, "are you going to stop paying tithe?" He didn't even hesitate, "No," he said "God's brought me this far, I'm going to keep paying the same amount of tithe and trust Him to work it out." Not even a week later, God sold the broken-up dock for the price he had originally asked. Now this friend always has money for tithes and offerings. He tested God, as God said to do, and God proved faithful.

I wonder why it is so difficult for us to part with a tithe—that's just ten-percent. Perhaps you say you don't have very much money. You may not realize it, but it's only by God's grace that you have what money you do

___
[8] Gal. 3:26-29
[9] Jas. 1:2-4

have. God owns everything. It all belongs to Him. He's asking you to give back to him a small amount of what He gave you.

If you have $10.00, you owe God $1.00. If you have $20.00, you owe God $2.00. Just remove the last zero and move the decimal point one place to the left. You will know exactly how much you owe—and you do owe it. God is a gracious God but He does want you to get started on getting things right with Him. Start with what you know you can give and ask Him to bless it and help you be able to pay a full tithe. If you are sincere, He will do it. Getting right with God will require you to take a step of faith. If your faith is no bigger than a grain of mustard seed, then start there but be consistent and faithful. If your children are just learning to honor God with their first fruit, they owe one penny for every ten-cents.

Perhaps you will want to look at your lifestyle to see if there are areas where you could cut back to help you pay tithe. Some items that come to mind: cigarettes, alcohol, soda, chips, dips and candies, the beauty salon...and you could probably add to the list. Perhaps your family could put their heads together to see what you would be willing give up in order to have God's blessing.

God says,

> Give and it shall be given to you
> Good measure pressed down,
> Shaken together,
> And running over
> Will be poured into your bosom.
> With the measure you use,
> It will be given to you.[10]

Final Thoughts on Tithe

Paying tithe is an indication of your heart commitment to Jesus. Jesus wants you to take advantage of the blessings that are yours when you are obedient.

---

[10] Lk. 6:38

Never give tithe just to get something from God—give tithe because of your gratitude for what Jesus has done for you. Give tithe because you understand that everything belongs to Him. Give tithe because you know that anything you have is because God allows you to have it.[11] Give because you want God's promised blessings so that you can bless others and be a "giver" and a "lender," You want to be debt-free—never again a slave to debt.

How many of us are guilty of going to church and managing to sit someplace where the offering plate won't be passed? Or going to church and when the offering plate is passed, pulling out a dollar, just because we feel we should give *something*.

The Apostle Paul's council was to determine how much you are going to give and then putting it aside, so that when it is time to give, you will have it ready.

If you give sparingly, you will reap sparingly. God says that the resources He gives you will slip away as if you put them into purses with holes.[12] If you sow generously, you will reap generously. Each one needs to make a heart decision, between you and Jesus, how much you are going to give. Don't give reluctantly or under pressure, for God loves a cheerful giver.[13] God is able to make all grace abound to you in all things at all times.

> The rich rule over the poor
> And the borrower is
> Slave to the lender.[14]

---

[11] Deut 8:17,18
[12] Hag. 1:5,6
[13] 2Cor. 9:7
[14] Prov. 22:7

Tithe Revisited

1. Did you take time to look up the study texts?
    All____ Some____ None____

2. Do you currently give 10% of your earnings back to God?
    Yes____ No____

3. Do you plan to? Yes____ No____

4. If not, have you ever considered that you are robbing God?
    Yes____ No____

5. Have you discussed tithing with your spouse? Yes____ No____

6. Will you discuss it together? Yes____ No____

7. Do you want God to abundantly bless your home and family?
    Yes____ No____

8. Is God prompting you to give up something so that you can pay him a full tithe? Yes____ No

9. What do you believe Jesus is prompting you to sacrifice for Him?_
    _____

10. Are you teaching your children to give money to God?
    Yes____ No____

Offerings are not discussed here; because, once you get your tithe right with God, He will help you to desire to give offerings, as well. And, you will be able to do it.

HEALING

Healing is for today and healing is for every Christian person.

The Apostle John, by The Holy Spirit wrote, "Beloved, I wish above all things that you will prosper and be in health, even as your soul, in Jesus Christ, is well and prospers."[1]

In the prophecy of Jesus' coming to earth to save us from sin, the Prophet Isaiah said, "...by His stripes we are healed..."[2] This prophecy had application when Jesus was here on earth, it has application for the present and it has a future application when Jesus takes His children Home. At that time there will be no more sickness or death.

When God came to earth clothed in skin,[3] He took up His earthly ministry at age 30 and immediately began healing the sick—in some instances He healed ALL that were sick. Sometimes He said, "...your faith has healed you."[4] At other times, He said nothing about faith, He just healed and faith came later.[5] When he visited His boyhood town of Nazareth, He expressed amazement at their lack of faith and The Bible records that He could only heal a few people.[6]

Jesus still heals today; but He heals in His way and at His time. We cannot tell Him how to do it. You will hear Word of Faith preachers tell you that it is not necessary to pray "...If it be Thy will..." Some present it as though praying "if it is God's will" in regard to healing is a sin! They use the text in Isaiah 53 to say that it is God's will for everyone to be healed all the time, every time and if you are not healed, you must have prayed wrong or lacked faith. DO NOT BELIEVE THIS. The Apostle Paul prayed to be healed of a physical affliction on three occasions. God did not heal Paul, but He encouraged him by telling him, "My grace is sufficient for you. My power

---

[1] 3Jn. 2
[2] Isa. 53:5
[3] Heb. 2:14-17
[4] Mt. 8:10; 9:2; Mk. 5:34
[5] Jn. 8:3ff
[6] Mk. 6:4-6

is made perfect in weakness."[7] If it was Jesus' plan to heal everybody all the time, He surely would have healed the Apostle Paul.

God declares that He is the Potter who created us and we are not to presume to tell Him what to do with His hands or His creation.[8]

Before Jesus went to the cross He prayed, "Let this cup pass from me; but not my will but Thine be done."[9] Jesus modeled for us how to pray in our extremity. If praying for God's will was good enough for Jesus, certainly it is good enough for us. The Bible says Jesus was heard because of His reverent submission.[10] I believe it's time we return to reverent submission.

I recommend you read the story of Job.[11] Job was afflicted with painful boils from the top of his head to the soles of his feet—The Bible says, he could only sit with a piece of broken pottery and scrape the pus off of his sores. His Friends came to "comfort" Job. They sat with Job for seven days and nights without saying a word. Sometimes that's all we need to do when making a comfort call, just sit in companionable silence. Anyway, at the end of the seven days and nights, Job's friends made up for all the good they had done by preceding to tell Job how he must have sinned, must have displeased God, must have robbed the poor and so on.

There are folks today who will tell you similar things: "If your kids are in trouble, if you are sick, if you're in financial hard times it's because something is wrong with *you*." That's why we need to always keep our eyes on Jesus, know His Word and keep our hearts tuned into Him.

Anyway, God finally spoke up and told Job's friends, "You have not spoken of Me right, as my servant Job has.[12] God commanded Job to pray for his friends who had failed him—you might want to remember that, when you feel misused or let down by your friends. Pray for them, this is intercessory

---

[7] 2Cor. 12:7-10
[8] Isa. 45:11; Rom. 9:21
[9] Lk.22:42
[10] Heb. 5:7
[11] Job 1-42
[12] Job .42:7

prayer.[13] As a result of Job's prayers, his friends were forgiven and Job's health and provision was restored to him.[14]

I had a friend who was diagnosed with kidney cancer. She and another friend immediately started her on a macrobiotic diet. If you don't know, that is a diet that incorporates great amounts of vitamins. There can be other components, too; but that's what they were doing. They testified to anyone who would listen that Jesus was going to perform a miracle to heal her. I said, "…but God has already performed a miracle: you only need ONE kidney to live. Have that diseased kidney removed!" Well, she didn't. The cancer in the kidney invaded her bladder and elsewhere and very soon she was dead. You cannot dictate to God how He is going to perform for you—He is not your trick monkey,

In Israel, my husband and I met a young man and his wife preparing to be baptized in the Jordan River, as Jesus had been. The man shared with us that he had been diagnosed with testicular cancer and his doctor strongly recommended surgery to remove the diseased testicle—but he believed God would heal him. The man proclaimed that when he went under the water, in baptism, Jesus would heal him of the cancer. Although one does not need testicles to live, he had prepared his unsaved family for this miracle that he felt sure God would perform. God did not heal him; but, God did allow him to see his beautiful newborn baby and hold her once before he died.

God, through His compassion for us, has provided means for us to be healed. Sometimes it is through doctors and medicine. Sometimes He performs an unexplainable miracle; at other times he allows us to die and takes us Home to be with Him. The Bible says good people die to prevent them from having to deal with things and circumstances which would be too difficult.[15]

I can suggest to you one important way that God promotes health and healing. God says we must forgive people who offend or harm us; for, only

---

[13] See Intercessory Prayer, pg.19
[14] Job 42:10ff; Jas. 5:16
[15] Isa. 57: 1,2; Ps. 116:15

then will He forgive us.[16] Healing and forgiveness go hand-in-hand. God tells us to confess our faults to each other and pray and forgive each other so we can be healed.[17] Harboring grudges is one of the most destructive activities in our lives. It causes poor health and even death. Unforgiveness and grudges are like a bucket filled with corrosive acid. It sloshes around and eats away at our insides, our peace of mind and wellbeing. When God tells us to forgive, it is more for us than for those we believe have sinned against us. Harboring anger and hostility harms us. God knows that hate and discontent erode and will eventually kill us—even eternally. Let me encourage you to forgive. There is nothing in this world worth hanging onto and missing out on Heaven.

Do you believe you just cannot forgive? God does not tell us to forgive one another in our own strength. We have Holy Spirit power to assist us to fulfill God's requirement—He gives us HIS strength.[18] We only need to pray and ask Him for it. God will supply His strength generously, without finding fault.[19]

Final thoughts on Healing

Yes, God heals today.

He heals in four ways: 1) He created our bodies to heal themselves; 2) He has instituted laws of science and medicine that, when followed, often result in physical or mental healing; 3) He performs unexplainable miracles and 4) He takes us Home to be with Him.[20]

Every one of these ways of healing is a miracle. The first three are temporary healings; that is, unless Jesus comes to take us Home, we will all eventually die. The fourth way is permanent healing, never again to deal with pain, sickness or death.

---

[16] Mt. 6:12;14,15
[17] Jas. 5:16
[18] Phil. 4:13
[19] Jas. 1:5
[20] Life after Death pg. 32

God will heal in any of these ways; but He has also given us steps to follow to request our healing. He says to anoint the sick with oil and pray sincerely for their healing. He doesn't say that this is only to be used in the event of catastrophic illness nor does He say that if we don't anoint with oil He will not heal. Following this prescription is an act of obedience. The anointing oil is representative of The Holy Spirit who actually does the healing. This procedure is appropriate for any illness situation: physical, mental, emotional or spiritual. We are told to call the elders of the church. Every Christian, who takes God's Word seriously, is a minister of The Gospel, an ambassador of Christ and responsible to minister as His representative. You are certainly able to anoint with oil[21] your Christian brother or sister and fervently pray in the Name of Jesus for their healing.[22] Be prepared to take up this responsibility all the more frequently in these last days when pastors and priests have abdicated and perverted their responsibilities before God.

We cannot dictate to God how or when He will heal—it is for Him to determine the work of His hands and His ways are not our ways. At the present time, we see through a glass darkly and know only part of any circumstance. One day, when we are with Christ, we will see Him face-to-face and know and understand, just as He does.[23]

Why are you so downcast, O my soul?
Why are you anxious?
My hope is in God!
I will continue to praise Him,
For He is my health.
He puts a smile on my face
And joy in my heart.[24]

A faithful ambassador is health.[25]

Pleasant words are as honeycomb:
sweet to the soul and health to the bones.[26]

---

[21] Mt. 25:1-13 (oil represents The Holy Spirit)
[22] Jas. 5:13-16
[23] 1Cor. 13
[24] Ps. 43:5
[25] Prov. 13:17
[26] Prov. 16:24

Healing Revisited

1. Did you take time to look up the study texts?
   All____ Some____ None____

1. Prior to this study, did you believe that healing is for today?
   Yes____ No____

2. Have you ever personally known someone who was healed unexpectedly? Yes____ No____

   If yes, who was it?_____

   How did that affect you?_____

3. Would you say it was a miracle? Yes____ No____

4. If No, how would you explain it?_____

5. Have you ever known anyone sick who was prayed for after being anointed with oil? Yes____ No____

6. Would you anoint with oil and pray for someone who needs healing? Yes____ No____ Maybe____

7. Could you explain to someone else the four ways that God heals?
   Yes____ No____

LIFE AFTER DEATH

Have you ever thought about what happens to us after we die? Are we worm-bait? Do we incarnate into another form or entity? Or do we reach nirvana, where we are blown-out like a candle? None is true.

As a child I received a lot of teaching about the state of the dead; but when I began studying this issue from the perspective of The Bible, I discovered some surprising facts. For one, I found that what I had been taught as a child was not biblically correct. Imagine my surprise to find I had gone through my life believing I knew all about it. I also discovered that this topic is of great interest to a lot of people—especially those suffering serious illness, the elderly and those who have lost loved ones. These events suddenly make the matter of life-after-death very important. I have received so many questions on this subject that I chose to find out for sure what The Bible has to say about it, to be certain my answers are truthful. It wasn't good enough to spout denominational rhetoric or feel-good platitudes or what someone else had told me. I wanted Bible truth. I wanted to know what God said. I'm so glad I didn't settle for less because a lot of questions were cleared up for me. Suddenly, I am able to rejoice when my Christian loved ones leave this earth—and, even rejoice with my own near death experiences—five in all.

In parochial school I learned two main texts to explain this phenomenon. I can still quote them from memory: "The living know that they shall die; but the dead know not anything. Neither have they anymore a reward forever in anything that is done under the sun. Their love and their hatred and their envy is now perished, for the former things are passed away..."[1] Well there is no sun in Heaven or The New Earth because The Bible says God, Himself is the Light[2]—so it makes perfect sense that they would have no participation in anything done under the sun. Also, before Jesus died on the cross, no one went to Heaven. Everyone remained in the grave (except Enoch,[3] Moses[4] and Elijah[5]—these were special circumstances).

---

[1] Eccl. 9:5.6
[2] Rev. 21:23
[3] Gen. 5:23,24
[4] Jude 9
[5] 2Ki. 2:1,11

The second text I learned was "His breath goes forth, he returns to the earth. In that very day his thoughts perish.[6] Well, we know that prior to Jesus death on the cross that's exactly what did happen. There was no possibility of eternal life until Jesus paid sin's price through His death on the cross and resurrection from the dead. That's why The Bible says that on the cross "He was put to <u>death in the body</u> but made <u>alive in The Spirit</u>, through whom He went and preached to the spirits in prison who disobeyed long ago..."[7] I've heard preachers scoff[8] and deny that Jesus preached to captives in hell; but since God said it, I believe it. Each of us will stand before the Judgement Seat of Christ to give an account of deeds done in the body[9] and those who presume to teach will be held to a higher accountability.[10]

After Jesus' returned to Heaven the Apostle Paul said, "If I am to go on living in the body, this will mean fruitful labor for me. Yet, what shall I choose? I do not know! I am torn between the two. I desire to depart and be with Christ, which is better by far."[11] Notice, he did not say he desired to depart and sleep in the grave.

Paul talks to us so we will not be ignorant about what happens to us or our loved ones. He says, just as Jesus resurrected from the dead, so we believe that when Jesus comes to gather us Home, <u>God will bring with Jesus those who have fallen asleep in Him. Jesus will come in the clouds and His church will be caught up to meet The Lord in the air.</u>[12] He says we will not get to Heaven before they do—Jesus will bring them with Him..."we will not precede them."

This appearance of Christ is not His second coming; it is not the end of the world. How do I know? Because, at The Second Coming of Christ, Jesus will come to this earth and His feet will rest on the Mount of Olives.[13] When Jesus comes to get those who love Him, He will not come to this earth. He will remain in the clouds and we, who love Him, will be "caught up" into

---

[6] Ps. 146:4
[7] Eph. 4:8-10; 1Pet 3:18-20
[8] Jude 17-19
[9] Rom. 14:11-12' 2Cor. 5:10
[10] Jas. 3:1
[11] Php. 1:22-23
[12] 1Th. 4:14-17
[13] Zech. 14:4

the clouds to be with Him"…and so shall we ever be with The Lord."[14] Some call this "catching away" the "rapture." The rapture could happen at any moment—we do not know the day or the hour. In fact, Jesus said The Master will return when we least expect Him.[15] We will be marrying, giving in marriage and having a high old time. He will come as a thief in the night.[16]

Everything from Revelation 5 through Revelation 20 will occur after the rapture of the saints. Through the Rapture of the saints God is fulfilling His promise to overcomers to keep them from the hour of trial[17] that is coming upon the whole earth. It will be a terrible time for the nation of Israel and for everyone on the earth who receives Jesus as Savior at that time. At the Second Coming of Jesus all the saints in Heaven (those raptured and those who died in The Lord) will accompany His return to earth[18] and every eye on earth will see Him[19]—the righteous and the wicked.

As I study Scripture, I understand that God does not change.[20] He told us He doesn't, so I believe we can use the analogy of birth to help us understand death with our subsequent birth into new life.

Consider the infant growing in its mother's womb—all warm, snuggly and well fed having all of its needs met. When the time for birth into this world comes, baby is squeezed and uncomfortable and may even hurt. If we could ask the baby at that stressful moment, "Do you want to go?" It would most likely cry, "No!" But, once baby is out of the birth canal and loving arms reach for it, that baby would never choose to return to its mother's womb. In fact, once out of the womb it has no memory of its birth womb and no longer communicates with it.

Likewise, we live and grow in the womb of this world. For the most part, it is good. We become comfortable, feel safe and our needs are met. THEN, comes the time to leave this world and we are squeezed, become

---

[14] 1Th. 4: 14-18 (note esp. v.17)
[15] Mt.24:50
[16] 1Th. 5:2,4
[17] Rev. 3:10
[18] Jude 14
[19] Rev. 1:7
[20] Mal. 3:6

uncomfortable and sometimes even hurt. Many would say, "I don't want to go!" But, when the Christian views his last sight in this world he opens his eyes in Heaven. We take our last breath of earthly air and the next breath is heavenly. As we travel the "birth canal" from this world, loving arms reach for us. Given the opportunity, we would never choose to return to the womb of the world. In Heaven, we have no further memory of, nor communication with, earthly things, people or events.

Those who believe their loved ones are watching or are somehow witnessing or involved in daily activities on this earth, are in grave error. I say "grave error" because such a belief sets one up to attempt to communicate with the dead, which will result in eternal death (see Angels, Demons and the Occult).

The Bible does say that we are surrounded by a great cloud of witnesses; but if you read that particular passage[21] you will see the word, "Therefore…" beginning verse one of chapter twelve. "Therefore," indicates that chapter twelve is being written because of the lives portrayed in chapter eleven. The lives of those individuals—and many more—are *witnessing to us*! We have nothing to share with them. They have already graduated this vale of tears and have gone on to the wonderful things God has prepared for them in Heaven.[22] The lives of those who have gone on before, witness to us of their obedience, their perseverance and their faithfulness under trial and God's faithfulness and care to them!

God has so many more wonderful things to show them! Perhaps they are learning about stars; visiting constellations; playing with beautiful, unblemished, fearless creatures; enjoying gorgeous unsullied flowers or tasting out-of-this world fruits and vegetables. Perhaps God is teaching them the mysteries of salvation.[23] The Bible says that even the angels long to understand the Plan of Salvation. One thing I can tell you for certain, we will not be spirits flitting from here to there or sitting on a cloud strumming a harp. The Bible says that now we see through a glass darkly because we only understand part of anything; but in Heaven, we will see face-to-face

---

[21] Heb. 12:1
[22] 1Cor. 2:9
[23] 1Pet 1:12Lp; Col. 2:2

and know even as God knows us.[24] God tells us further that we cannot even begin to imagine the wonderful things He has prepared for those who love Him.[25]

Final Thoughts on Life after Death

Suicide is not the unpardonable sin. Our Lord Jesus knows the mind and heart of all men and women and He judges accordingly. He takes into account physical, mental, emotional conditions, as well as one's heart relationship with Him. You can trust The Judge of all the earth to do right.[26]

Cremation is not a sin against God nor is it an abuse of a corpse. The body that is buried is not the body that will be raised. The body that is sown is perishable. The new body will be imperishable, incorruptible.[27] We will be changed in a moment; in the twinkling of an eye. The body that lies in the grave will disintegrate and rot, slowly returning to dust.[28] It really doesn't matter whether the body deteriorates slowly by decay or quickly by fire. The deceased will not use this old body[29] again; and he or she is not in the grave[30] awaiting your visits and decorations. Christians are with Jesus. Cremation is a personal decision; but it is not a sin.

> I know not now how soon 'twill be
> When I shall reach that vast unknown.
> I know not now, I cannot see
> The entrance to the heavenly home.
> Alas, alas 'tis better so,
> For time moves on with rapid pace.
> But this I know, when I shall go,
> That I shall see Him face-to-face!
> For life must come and life must go,
> The winters pass the spring flowers grow;

---

[24] 1Cor. 13:12
[25] 1Cor. 2:9 (repeat)
[26] Gen. 18:25Lp
[27] 1Cor. 15:42; 51,52; 2Cor.5:1-8
[28] Gen. 3:19
[29] 2Cor. 4:7
[30] Php. 1:21-23

And though this bliss be but alloy,
'Tis less of pain with more of joy.
It matters not a few years more,
It matters not how quick the pace
For this I know: on that fair shore,
I will see Him face-to-face.
Yes, I shall see Him face-to-face
And be with those I love once more;
Yes, I shall see Him face-to-face
And be with Him forevermore.[31]

What happens to those who die without receiving Jesus as Savior?

Most of us know people who have died not believing in Jesus. Interestingly, God also tells us what happens to the wicked when they die. You might be thinking, "But, these people were not wicked; they were good people, they just didn't believe in Jesus."

God doesn't view people as we do. He doesn't judge by what He sees on the outside.[32] God looks at the heart. Man's ultimate wickedness is to not receive and trust Jesus Christ as personal Savior and Lord.[33]

Most people want to believe that we all go to Heaven when we die and we don't like to think that anyone is going to hell. According to Scripture, even professing Christians will not go to Heaven, if they do not have a sincere heart relationship with Jesus.[34]

The Bible tells us the unmistakable truth: the wicked die and they do not live again until the end of all things. At that time, they will stand before the white throne judgment and will be cast into the Lake of Fire.[35]

---

[31] Face-to-Face; Herbert Johnson 1898
[32] 1Sam 16:7
[33] Ac 4:12; Rom 10:9-13
[34] Mt. 7:21-23
[35] Rev 20:12-15; 1Cor.6:9,10

God so loved the world that He gave His only begotten Son
That whosoever believes on Him will have everlasting life…
Whoever believes on Jesus is not condemned;
But whoever does not believe on Him stands condemned already
Because he has not believed in the Name
of God's one and only Son.[36]

---

[36] Jn. 3:16, 18

Life after Death in Review

1. Did you take time to check out the study texts?
   ___All ___Some ___None

2. Before reading this chapter, what did you believe happened at death? _____

   _____

3. Have your thoughts on suicide and cremation changed?
   Yes___ No___

4. Did you believe the righteous and the wicked had the same destiny?
   Yes___ No___

5. How do you feel now that you know what The Bible says?_____

   _____

6. Are you thinking of friends and loved ones with whom you want to share Jesus, before it's too late? Write their names here_____

   _____

7. Could you explain Life after death to someone else? Yes___ No___

Did you ever wonder: "If God is such a loving God, why did He send <u>His Son</u> to die for us? How does sending one's son to die define a loving God? I remember hearing a story when I was a child. A father had his son stick his finger into a dyke to prevent flooding. Of course, the water rose over the son's head and he died; but many people were saved.[1] The justification was that many people were saved. I never thought that was a very loving action on the part of his father; nor did I think it was a loving action on the part of Father God to send His Son to die for our sins.

Did you ever try to rationalize The Trinity? Perhaps you said, "Well, if God is The Father and Jesus is The Son then The Holy Spirit must be the Mother." Don't laugh. As a child I tried to rationalize it in just that way. I was attempting to make God fit into what in the world I understood and no one was telling me any different. I realize now that those I asked weren't really sure how all this worked either. I'm sure some of you have treated The Bible similarly. In an attempt to make sense out of a concept that you found difficult to understand, you allowed your mind to create its own explanation. I believe, human nature is to try to make God and His Word fit into what we understand. The good news is The Bible has the answers.[2]

Do you believe that Jesus first came into being at the virgin birth? Do you believe Jesus is a creation of God, just as we are creations of God and, by that fact, is our brother? Perhaps you take that idea a step farther and believe that Jesus is a creation of God just as Satan is a creation of God and, therefore, Jesus and Satan are brothers. There are religious groups who teach both of these concepts.

I want to help you unravel this mystery. The answer lies in understanding what Scripture refers to as the *Mystery of God*. The only way to understand it is to allow The Bible to give us the answer and take God at His Word. Here's a hint: one of Jesus' names is *Immanuel*, which means: "God with us." The Apostle John clearly tells us, "The Word became flesh and dwelt among us...He was in the world and though the world was made through Him, the world did not recognize Him..." Too many of us take <u>one</u> verse

---

[1] A corrupt telling of a children's story
[2] 2Tim. 3:15-17

from Scripture and never look any further to see just how the pieces fit together. It's time we study all of the texts on the subject and take God at His Word. Following are a few declarations from Scripture:

> For unto us a child is born, unto us a son is given...and his Name shall be called Wonderful Counselor, Almighty God, Everlasting Father, Prince of Peace.[3]

> Now to Him who is able to establish you by The Gospel proclaimed of Jesus Christ; according to the revelation of The Mystery hidden for long ages past, but now revealed and made know through the prophetic writings by the command of The eternal God, so that all nations might believe and obey Him—to the only wise God be glory forever through Jesus Christ! Amen,[4]

> And He made known to us The Mystery of His will according to His good pleasure, which He purposed in Christ, to be put into effect when the times will have reached fulfillment—to bring all things in Heaven and on earth together under one Head, even Christ.[5]

> The Apostle Paul said, I have become servant (to the church) by the commission God gave me to present to you The Word of God in its fullness—The Mystery that has been kept hidden for ages and generations, but is now disclosed to the saints. To them, God has chosen to make known among the Gentiles the glorious riches of this Mystery which is Christ in you, the hope of glory. We proclaim Him, admonishing and teaching everyone with all wisdom, so that we may present everyone perfect in Christ.[6]

---

[3] Isa. 9:6
[4] Rom. 16:25-27
[5] Eph. 1:9,10
[6] Col. 1:25-28

And pray for us, that God may open a door for our message, so that we may proclaim The Mystery of Christ, for which I am in chains. Pray that I may proclaim it clearly.[7]

To Him who is able to keep you from falling and to present you before His glorious presence without fault and with great joy—to the only God, our Savior, be glory, majesty, power and authority through Jesus Christ Our Lord— before all ages, now and forevermore! Amen.[8]

About the Son He says, "In the beginning, O Lord, You laid the foundations of the earth and the heavens are the work of Your hands. They will perish, but You will remain; they will wear out like a garment. You will roll them up like a robe; like a garment they will be changed; but You remain the same and Your years will never end.[9]

The Revelation of Jesus Christ which God gave Him to show His servants what must soon take place. I am The Alpha and The Omega, says the Lord God, who is and who was and who is to come—The Almighty.[10]

Then the angel I had seen standing on the sea and on the land raised his right hand to Heaven. And he swore by Him who lives forever and ever, who created the heavens and all that is in them, the earth and all that is in it and the sea and all that is in it and said, "There will be no more delay! But in the days when the seventh angel is about to sound his trumpet, The Mystery of God will be accomplished, just as He announced to his servants the prophets."[11]

Did you ever wonder why such a fuss is made over anyone speaking or praying in the Name of Jesus? We can pray in the name of Allah, also

---

[7] Col. 4:3-5
[8] Jude 24-25
[9] Heb. 1:10-12
[10] Rev. 3:1,8
[11] Rev. 10:5-7

known as the moon god, in whose name devout followers commit jihad and intifada; Moloch and Baal, in whose names children were burned in the fire; Ishtar, worshiped as the god who promotes fertility, sexual love and war; the Queen of Heaven, called Isis, Astarte, Asherah and Roman Catholics call her Mary the mother of Jesus; the sun god, which was various deities representing the sun; and on and on--god may even be your refrigerator, a new car, a sporting event, alcohol, cigarettes or your convenience. But, when you talk about Jesus, that's specific! Jesus is THE GOD of Heaven and earth. He is The Master Designer, He can change your life; He can save your soul![12]

There is power in the Name of Jesus! That's why the leaders of the synagogue commanded Peter and John: "...not to speak or preach at all in The Name of Jesus..."[13] That is why Satan has attempted, ever since, to stop those who speak in Jesus' Name. There is a devil loose! He is determined to deceive even the elect[14] of Christ, if that is possible. We are not surprised, then, that even professed Christians stumble over The Name of Jesus—God's Word predicted this.[15]

The Name of Jesus is the "touch stone" to determine the faithfulness of our teachings and beliefs. Many sincere theologians stumble over Jesus' identity—proclaiming that He is not God Almighty. Some say, *He is God*-and they supply a nonverbal emphasis that implies: but not THE GOD. Some find it more comfortable to say He is "divine" which would give Him the rank of a god. Many Christians, if questioned closely, would uncomfortably attest to believing in *three* Gods: The Father, The Son and The Holy Spirit. They would be uncomfortable explaining just how all these pieces fit together; but they would firmly assert that God the Father is the Creator. Perhaps they would be comfortable to say that Jesus died on the cross and, maybe, for our sins—but maybe not. They might identify The Holy Spirit as our conscience. Scripture says "God is ONE.[16]

Scripture says Jesus is The Creator of the world and He created you and me.[17] Hebrews says God is spirit; but because the children (that's us) have

---

[12] Pray Jesus' Name page 20; footnotes 88-92
[13] Ac. 4:17,18
[14] Mt. 24:24
[15] Rom. 9:33; Isa. 8:14-15
[16] Deut. 6:4; Mk. 12:29; 1Tim. 2:5; Jas. 2:19
[17] Jn. 1:3,4,10,11; Heb. 1:8-12

flesh and blood, He put on flesh and blood[18] in order to be born in the same way that you and I are born.

Some of us believe Jesus first appeared on the scene when He was born of Mary, was wrapped in swaddling clothes and laid in a manger. According to Scripture, He is "The First and The Last"[19]—without generation or length of days.[20] Jesus is The Great I Am.[21]

Triune God
Glory cloud, Jesus, Holy Spirit dove

---

[18] Heb. 2:14,15
[19] Rev. 1:17;
[20] Heb. 7:1-3
[21] Ex. 3:14; Mk. 14:62; Rev. 1:8; 22:13

As Luke tells The Gospel story, the angel appeared to Mary to announce Jesus' impending birth and said, "The Holy One to be born will be *called* The Son of God."[22]

The Apostle John wrote, "He came unto His own; but His own would not receive Him."[23]

Jesus said, "If you believed Moses, you would believe Me, for Moses wrote about Me.[24] But, since you do not believe what he wrote, how are you going to believe what I say?" About what or whom did Moses write? He wrote about God leading the Children of Israel, parting the Red Sea, sending water from the Rock, providing bread ("manna") from Heaven and God saving them in conflict and so much more.[25]

Perhaps you are so caught up in your own humanity that you consign God to function within our human parameters—we need to settle that right now. God is before ALL. He can take any form He chooses and be in any place and everyplace. While being baptized, He can speak from Heaven and appear in the form of a dove. He is not bound by our earthy parameters. It doesn't matter if we understand it and, as a matter-of-fact, we won't understand fully until we get to Heaven. Let this be your refrain, "He is God and I am not." Repeat that as many times as you need to, until you finally get it. Understand this: He can do whatever He wants to do—and He will do exactly that, with or without our permission. He is The Great I AM—in other words, He will be anything and all that He chooses to be and all that we need. He put it very succinctly when He said, "I AM who I AM" and we can't say it any better.

Once that becomes reality within you, you begin to understand that God is more than able to step out of His Spirit-self, leave His eternal knowledge behind, implant Himself into the womb of a woman He created, suckle at her breast and be completely dependent upon her for His physical needs. Imagine it! The Creator of the universe! In fact, He did just that! He was born through the birth canal just as you and I were born and He grew

---

[22] Lk. 1:32.35
[23] Jn. 1:10,11
[24] Jn.5:46
[25] Ex. 1:1-40:38

in subjection to earthly parents He created! He grew in favor with God and man. He lived as created beings lived and walked the roads they walked—but, without sin. He took up His earthly ministry at age thirty. For three years he touched the untouchable, healed the unhealable, loved the unloveable and ultimately went to the cross to pay the penalty for your sins and mine. The Bible says He did this for the joy set before Him: The joy of seeing you and me restored to relationship with Him, conformed to His likeness and brought into communion and fellowship with Him. What a man! What a God! What a Savior!

Every one of us has sinned and sin's penalty is eternal death. There is nothing you or I could ever do to satisfy the sin debt. Only the sinless Creator could pay the price. He willingly chose to take all of our sins upon Himself and die in our place! The Bible says The Plan of Salvation was laid out before Jesus ever made the world. He knew we would sin and need a Savior. At that time, He chose to be our Savior, be born an infant and be *called* the Son of God. That makes all the difference to me—God didn't send His son, as you and I have sons. He chose to become The Son and be the blood sacrifice that would save us from our sins.

Perhaps you've wondered why God didn't just wipe Adam and Eve off the face of the earth and start over. I have. I found the answer in Scripture! Here it is: Because God is a covenant-keeping God. There were more people involved in that covenant than just Adam and Eve. God made a covenant with you and me when He chose us before He put the foundations of the world into place.[26]

We didn't even know about the covenant—but God did. He knew you and He committed to die for you, before He laid the foundations of the earth. He did this to restore you to relationship with Him. All He asks in return is that you accept His free gift by repenting of your sins and being baptized[27] into His Name.

Perhaps you would like to receive Jesus Christ as your Savior but don't know how. Simply and sincerely pray the following prayer:

---

[26] Jn. 15:16; Eph. 1:4,5; 2Th 2:13; Jas. 1:18
[27] See section on Sacraments: Baptism, pg. 114

Dear Lord,
I come humbly before you acknowledging that I am a sinner.
Please forgive my sins.
(name any that you remember)
Please cover my sins with Your precious blood
and save me.
In Jesus Name I pray.
Amen

As God has graced me with the ability to study His Word, He has placed on my heart a desire to help you understand this Mystery. I believe it's even more critical now as we enter turbulent and uncertain times. We <u>must</u> have an unwavering, confident understanding of our Great, Eternal God. Once you understand this Mystery, you will have a much greater appreciation and gratitude for what God did for your salvation.

To that end, I have written this to you. Not three Gods, but three presentations of ONE God. You will notice as you study The Father, The Son and The Holy Spirit, the lines begin to blur—because The Triune God is ONE God. This is why John the Revelator fell at Jesus' feet "as though dead"[28]—because of the astounding realization of the actual identity of his Friend, Jesus. The Book of Revelation is "The Revelation of Jesus Christ"[29]—therein, The Mystery of God is revealed.[30]

It is my prayer that you will be blessed as you prayerfully read and study. Be blessed as The Holy Spirit of God—The Holy Spirit of Jesus helps you to His understanding of The Triune God.

Final Thoughts on One Triune God

The preceding is not an exhaustive study on The Triune God. The Bible has much more to teach you. I invite you to look up the study passages to increase your knowledge of what The Bible says. It's impossible to study The Bible by jumping out of bed, allowing it to fall open and reading a verse

---

[28] Rev. 1:17,18
[29] Rev. 1:1
[30] Rev. 10:7

of two. Detailed Bible study takes some time because you need to pray for God's guidance through His Holy Spirit, then take a topic or word and find all of the places in Scripture where it occurs.

Keep notes and memorize, if you can; if you are unable to memorize, trust God to bring Scripture to your memory when you need it. This process will take longer but it is extremely rewarding. Some of The Bible software programs that are out now can make your study easier.

God has appointed some men and women with the gifts of preaching and teaching; but, when you seriously begin to study The Bible, The Holy Spirit will come alongside and open God's Word to you—you just have to ask Him. Very soon, you will be a stellar Bible scholar.

One Triune God in Review

1. Did you take time to check out the study texts?
   ___All ___Some ___None

2. Before studying this chapter, what did you believe about

   a. God The Father_____

   b. God The Son _____

   c. God The Holy Spirit _____

3. Does knowing who Jesus is change your feelings about His sacrifice for you? Yes___ No___

4. Could you explain The Triune God to someone else? Yes___ No___

God's Sovereign Choice
Our God is in Heaven;
He does whatever pleases Him[1]

As human beings, we find it difficult to understand that God does whatever He pleases and that what He pleases doesn't always coincide with what pleases us. This concept is especially hard to swallow if you've lived for your own pleasure and think everything should go your way. It's difficult if we have bought into the world's tolerance philosophy. It's difficult to comprehend that God isn't going to consider a "fairness doctrine" before administering His justice.

We all know the story of Jacob and Esau. Jacob's name means to "supplant" or "deceive." Why? Because when he was born he came out of the womb grasping his older twin's heel. Esau, whose Name means "red" was named for the red hair that covered his body at birth and throughout his life. Esau was robust and wild, and his father loved him. As he grew older he loved to hunt and would often make a savory stew for his father, from wild game he caught. Jacob was smooth-skinned and had a more mild temperament and stayed around the family compound. Rebekah loved him. She often remembered what God had told her: "The older will serve the younger."

Rebekah wanted Jacob to have his father's birthright blessing and she probably talked to Jacob about it frequently from the time he was little. In those days, receiving the patriarch's birthright blessing was a major deal. It meant blessings from God, honor and esteem in the family and inheriting the majority of the father's wealth. As the twins grew older, Jacob looked for ways to scam his brother out of his birthright. One day Esau, who loved to hunt, came in famished from the fields. Jacob was cooking red lentil stew and Esau pleaded for some. Jacob agreed, but only on the condition that Esau would sell to him his birthright. Esau cared so little for the birthright—actually, The Bible says he despised it—that he readily agreed, "What do I care about an old birthright—I'm starving!" and he wolfed-down the stew. Since the stew he bought was red, he was given the name Edom. Subsequently, his land was known as Edom and his descendants as Edomites.

---

[1] Ps. 115:3

No doubt you feel a little sorry for Esau and a little ticked at Jacob. But the Bible says that while the boys were still in their mother's womb and had done nothing good or bad, God chose Jacob and gave him preference over Esau. Actually, The Bible records that God told their mother "The older will serve the younger." It is recorded that before the twins were born God said, "Jacob I loved; but Esau I hated."[2] God did this to make it understood that He does what He wants to do and operates by His choice—not according to what someone does or doesn't do. Probably, all of the things which occurred between Jacob and Esau would have been accomplished in God's way, if mother had kept her fingerprints off of the situation. On the other hand, nothing that was done was a surprise to God. He is omniscient.

We often tell the story of Israel's deliverance from bondage in Egypt.[3] It was a story often repeated by the disciples in the first century church. We tell the story of Moses and Aaron going to speak to Pharaoh, the ruler of Egypt to negotiate Israel's release. Many of us have memorized the order of the plagues God brought on the land of Egypt, because of Pharaoh's hard heart. We have discussed his stubbornness and marveled that it took him so long to learn his lesson. At one time, God brought a plague of frogs on the land and frogs were in the kneading troughs and in everyone's beds. Pharaoh called Moses and Aaron and said, "Pray to the Lord so He will take these frogs out of here!" Moses said, "Alright. When do you want me to pray?" We were amazed to read Pharaoh's reply. "Tomorrow," he said.[4] We know that the final plague was the death angel that passed over Egypt at midnight and killed every firstborn son, from the palace to the homes and even servants. The Bible says the firstborn of livestock died, as well.[5] We think, "What a tragedy that it took Pharaoh so long to give in to The Lord!"

Would it surprise you to know that the Apostle Paul tells us that Pharaoh behaved that way because God hardened his heart.[6] God did this in order to display His power in Pharaoh and so that His Name would be proclaimed throughout the earth.[7] It was.

---

[2] Gen. 25:21-34; Mal. 1-5; Rom. 9:10-13
[3] Ex. 1:1-12:50
[4] Ex. 8:1-10
[5] Ex. 11 & 12
[6] Rom 9:16-18
[7] Ibid

Do you think God is unfair? God is The Potter, we are just the clay. He has a word for you:

"Who are you, O man to talk back to God.[8]
"Shall what is formed say to Him who formed it,
'Why did You make me like this?'
"Doesn't The Potter have the right
"to make whatever He wants from the clay?
"So what, if I want to show my wrath
"and so I make objects for wrath--
"prepared in advance for destruction?
"So what if I did this to make known
"the riches of My glory to vessels
"I formed in advance for honor?
"Those I have called from
"Jews and Gentiles."
"I will have mercy
on whomever I choose to have mercy
and I will have compassion
for those on whom I choose to have compassion."[9]

Judas, the disciple who betrayed Jesus was prepared in advance for destruction[10] There have been several, whose stories are told in Scripture, who were obviously prepared in advance for destruction. There are many who were prepared in advance for mercy. If you love the Lord Jesus, you were prepared in advance for mercy. Jesus said He chose us before he laid the foundations of the world.[11] When He prayed in The Garden of Gethsemane, he prayed for His disciples and those that He had chosen. He says specifically, I am not praying for the world.[12] Do you believe it is not fair that some are chosen for honor and some for dishonor? Well, if you love Jesus, He chose you for honor—and that's not fair either, but I'm so very glad He did!

---

[8] Isa. 45:11-12; Rom. 9:19-25
[9] Rom. 9:14,15
[10] Jn. 17:12; Ac.1:16-20
[11] Eph. 1:4-6
[12] Jn. 17:6-15

God says that before He formed us in the womb, He calls us by name and sets us apart for a purpose.[13]

God has chosen the small things, the weak and despised things of this world to show forth His glory. So that no one can boast before Him.[14]

You and I don't know who He has chosen and so we preach The Gospel to everyone. God knows who belongs to Him and He will faithfully sort it out. In the meantime we need to stop second-guessing Him and passing judgement on Him. Shall not The Judge of all the earth do right?[15]

Surely, as I have planned, so it will be
And as I have purposed, so it will stand.[16]
Repeat after me:
God is God and I am not

---

[13] Jer. 1:5
[14] 1Cor. 1:28
[15] Ge. 18:25
[16] Isa. 14:24

God's Sovereign Choice Revisited

1. Did you take time to check out the study texts?
    ___ All ___ Some ___ None

2. Were you surprise that before a child is born, God knows that child, calls it by name and has planned its destiny? Yes___ No___

3. Are you angry with God? Yes___ No___

4. Are you angry because He didn't choose everyone? Yes ___ No ___

5. Do you believe He has the right to decide what He does with the clay? Yes ___ No___

6. Are you angry that He chose you? Yes___ No___

7. Are you angry because your church has chosen not to believe Him? Yes___ No___

8. If you are angry, God knows that and He can handle your anger. Go talk to Him about it.

The Mark

Many Christians go about today, afraid some world power is going to make them take the Mark of the Beast. We hear that we will be forced to have an identifying chip placed under the skin in our hand or arm. Businesses, institutions and the government, it is said, will use this chip to know whether or not to allow us to buy or sell. Some have gone so far as to buy stock in such chips hoping to get rich when this mandate comes down.

Another possibility is a chip placed into the driver's license, credit cards, computers and even product codes on groceries and GPS systems in our phones and cars. We already have these chips so some believe it's just a matter of time until they morph into THE mark. We have very quickly advanced technologically and have trackable health records and bank accounts. Some have chosen not to own computers, TVs, GPS and such to prevent government snooping.

The Bible says the mark will be on our forehead or on our hand.[1] This has given rise to some pretty interesting sci-fi books and movies.

And so, Christians go about wringing their hands and wondering just when and how all of these tactics will be used against us. God said He didn't come to give us a spirit of fear but instead the power of love and a sound mind.[2] He also commands us not to worry[3]—He's got everything under control. It's pretty difficult to be loving, and living in peace, while we're running around afraid of our shadows and looking over our shoulders to see how the devil is going to get us.

We can have a sound mind when we know God's Word. I have discovered that God never does anything without giving us an example beforehand. In the case of the Mark of the Beast, it is important first to understand The Mark of God. In His Word, God told us clearly what His mark is.

God gave a vision to His prophet, Ezekiel. In this vision, Ezekiel heard God call the priest (a man wearing linen) and tell him to go throughout the city

---

[1] Rev. 13:16
[2] 2Tim. 1:7
[3] Mt. 6:25-34

and place a mark on the forehead of everyone who grieves and weeps over the despicable things that are done in the land. God told him to start at the temple altar. Then He called the soldiers and told them to follow the priest and utterly kill, without pity, those who do not have The Mark: old men, old women, young men, young women and little children—but, He said, "don't touch anyone who has The Mark."[4]

Can you imagine that? Everyone without The Mark of God was killed—it didn't matter who they were. The soldiers were told to "slay without pity." That goes against the tolerance preached in this country. I hasten to assure you that God is not telling us to take these matters into our own hands today; but, one day, He will do it. Once again, I believe He will begin in our churches, cathedrals, temples and synagogues. He will begin at our pulpits, where preachers and priests are either declaring The Word of God—or not. His judgement on that day will be without pity.

God says He does not change.[5] Therefore, His Mark is the same today. Those who truly love The Lord will grieve over the despicable things done in our nation and around the world. If that is God's Mark, then it would stand to reason that Satan's mark, The Mark of the Beast, would be just the opposite: foolish talk, course joking and reveling in the debauchery, hedonism and immorality of this nation and the world. Love for the world and all that it does is hatred toward God.[6]

The mark on the forehead, I believe, is knowing, willful agreement or participation in the sins of the world. The mark in the hand denotes one who panders and promotes the sins of this world.

Final Thoughts on The Mark

The numerical mark of man is 666, his slogan is, "If it feels good, do it."

You see, while Satan forces those who love the world to take his mark, it will be accomplished through individual choices. Our heart condition will

---

[4] Ezk. 9
[5] Mal. 3:6; Jas. 1:17;
[6] 1Jn. 2:15.16; Gal. 5:19-21; Eph. 5:3--7

allow our master, whether Christ or Satan, to imprint the appropriate mark onto our forehead or into our hand. If your heart belongs to Jesus, you will wear The Mark of God. If your heart belongs to the world, you will wear the Mark of the Beast. The choice is yours alone.

Many individuals throughout history have been named The Beast or The Antichrist. In my few years on this planet, Hitler, Stalin, The collective Roman popes, Henry Kissinger, John F. Kennedy, Barak Obama, Hillary Clinton, Donald Trump, George Soros and many others have had their names put forth. The truth is, The Bible says The Antichrist is coming and many antichrists have already come.[7] Anyone who denies Jesus is the Christ or denies that He will return in the flesh is an antichrist.[8] I imagine you can think of some antichrists that you know.

We really do not have to go around fearful of chips and such or afraid that voting for this one or that one is going to bring the Antichrist. The Antichrist will come, no matter what we do and God declares that He sets up kings and rulers and takes them down.[9] So, VOTE! If Christians had exercised their God-given right to vote the world might not be in such a state today. Vote your conscience. Live your life being in this world but not of it and let the peace of God rule in your hearts.[10]

Hopefully, understanding better The Mark of the Beast will help you examine your own life to see if you have given any place to that mark. God wants to help us live for Him—without fear.

---

[7] 1Jn. 2:18
[8] 2Jn 7
[9] Dan. 2:20-22; 4:34,35
[10] Php. 4:7

Mark of the Beast in Review

1. Did you take time to check out the study texts?
    ___All ___Some ___None

2. What did you believe about the Mark of the Beast prior to reading this lesson?_____

    _____

3. How do you feel about The Bible's revelation of The Mark of God?

    _____

4. Does it make sense to you that The Mark of the Beast would be just the opposite of The Mark of God? Yes___ No___

5. Whose Mark do you wear?_____

6. Would you be able to explain The Mark of God and the Mark of the Beast to someone else? Yes___ No___

JUDGE...OR NOT?

Didn't Jesus say, "Do not judge or you will be judged? It's interesting to note how often people grab onto catchy phrases and never look any further to get the whole story.

Yes, Jesus said something like that, but we need to note to whom He was talking and the context of that discussion. Jesus came to the people of Israel. They were all God-fearing, devout people. They had been living by the Ten Commandments for generations. Those commandments had been passed down and practiced from Moses through the patriarchs and family lines. At the time of Jesus' earthly ministry He found His people sorely pressed by the religious leaders who were adding their own rules to those of God. Not only that, but the judgmental climate was such that people were critical of everything they saw others doing. It set up a tattle-tale mentality that caused suspicion and strife among neighbors, families and friends: their God-fearing brothers and sisters.

Jesus said to this careworn group, "Do not judge because you will be judged by the same measure you use to judge others.[1] This was a specific message to those who know God and do their best to live according to His standards. People were mind-weary and overburdened with rules and regulations and so Jesus told them not to judge one another.

He is saying the same thing to us today. Do not judge your Christian brothers and sisters on behaviors about which God has said nothing. In one of the classes I taught on discipleship, a gentleman told how he had been a collector of 45-records. He had quite a collection and he was very proud of it. Over a period of time, he began to feel that God was telling him he needed to get rid of those 45-records and eventually, he did. But then, he began telling others his story and adding that it was wrong to collect things--everyone needed to get rid of their collections. Now, this becomes a whole different story. Because he heard God tell him to get rid of his 45-record collection, I applaud him for doing so. Possibly, these records had become an idol to him so that he was in danger of forfeiting relationship with Jesus in order to maintain his record collection. He did the right thing to get them out of his life.

---

[1] Mt. 7:1-4

From time-to-time, God will show you and me the need to change things specific to us. But we cannot presume to apply that same decision to everyone, because The Bible doesn't speak to it. We are told not to have idols or gods before The Lord and He will convict us if we have them.

The story of the rich young man[2] comes to mind. God had a specific conversation with him about what he needed to do in order to be saved. At the end of the story, Jesus told him to sell all that he possessed and give the money to the poor. Some have chosen to believe that Jesus was saying it is wrong for Christians to have wealth or possessions. That is obviously not what Jesus was saying because The Bible has many stories of how God blessed individuals with great wealth.

Jesus the Judge
Jesus blindfolded with judgment scales

---

[2] Mt. 19:16-23

Sadly, the outcome of Jesus' direction to the young man was that the man went away sorrowful because he had many possessions; and therein was the crux of the problem. God told the young man to sell everything and give to the poor because his money and possessions were his idol. They meant more to him than his relationship with God, more to him than his salvation.[3]

The problem today is, we have a lot of people who profess to be Christian who do not know what that means, have no working knowledge of the text book or simply have chosen to live contrary to God's standards.

Jesus certainly didn't mean that we should never make any judgments. If so, His Word would never tell us:

1. Don't give what is sacred to dogs; do not throw your pearls to pigs[4]...they will trample you and tear you to pieces. This requires us to make a judgement as to what is sacred and who will treat them as such and what constitutes pearls and who are pigs and dogs who will trample them under foot or tear us to pieces.

2. Do not worry but leave everything to our Heavenly Father.[5] This requires a conscious judgement that worry is self-defeating, we can't change anything, only God can and to make the subsequent choice to leave the outcome to Him.

3. Do not say your prayers or give your charity to be seen of men.[6] This requires a conscious judgement as to whether we will choose to please God or man.

4. The spiritual man or woman judges everything.[7] All things must be viewed through the lens of Scripture[8]—that is the only way we can make right judgements.

---

[3] 1Tim. 6:10
[4] Mt. 7:6
[5] Mt. 6:25-34
[6] Mt. 6:5-14
[7] 1Cor. 2:15
[8] 2Tim. 3:15-17

5. God tells us not to discriminate or show favoritism[9]—this requires making a judgement about our attitudes and subsequently our choices.

Of course God wants us to be aware of what is happening with our Christian brothers and sisters and He directs us to speak out when there is sin, so that they can change their ways and be saved.[10] I am not speaking here about the Spirit-led man or woman who falls and immediately repents; for all have sinned and come short of God's glory.[11] I am speaking of one who willfully chooses to live contrary to God's law as an ongoing practice.[12]

Once we have accepted Jesus as our Savior, God expects us to work out our own salvation with fear and trembling[13]—that is, to live daily for His glory and to ensure that our lifestyle and behavior reflects Jesus Christ. We are Christ's ambassadors.[14]

The topic of judgement brings us to the place where it would be appropriate to take our own spiritual inventory to verify our heart condition before Jesus Christ.[15]

> "The acts of the sinful nature are obvious: sexual immorality, impurity and debauchery, idolatry and witchcraft, hatred, discord, jealousy, fits of rage, selfish ambition, dissensions, factions and envy, drunkenness, orgies and the like. I warn you…that those who live like this will not inherit the Kingdom of God."[16]

> "Among you there must not be even a hint of sexual immorality or of any kind of impurity or of greed; because these are improper for God's holy people. Nor should there be obscenity, foolish talk or coarse joking, which are out of place. Of this you can be sure, no immoral, impure

---

[9] Ac. 10:34; Rom. 2:11; Eph. 6:9; Col. 3:25; Jas. 2:1-12 (esp. v.9)
[10] Ezk. 33:7-20
[11] Rom. 3:23
[12] 1 Cor. 5:11,12
[13] Php. 2:12,13
[14] 2Cor. 5:20
[15] Mt. 7:3-5
[16] Gal. 5:19-21

or greedy person has any inheritance in the Kingdom of Christ and of God."[17]

"The fruit of the spirit is thankfulness, love, joy, peace patience, kindness, goodness, faithfulness; gentleness and self-control...since we live by The Spirit, let us keep in step with The Spirit."[18]

Final Thoughts on Judging

We are to frequently take our own spiritual inventory to know how we measure up to God's biblical standard. Once we have taken our personal spiritual inventory, God will let us know if we are ready to speak to our Christian brother or sister about his or her life. We are our brother's keeper. As we seek the mind of Christ, He will give us His love for one another and we will truly want the best for our fellow Christians. When we are functioning at God's direction and we don't know what to say or how to say it, His Holy Spirit will give us the words, *while we are speaking.* We will be willing to speak out if we see Christians living contrary to God's law, because we know the end of sin is death.[19] God tells us how to restore our loved ones to spiritual health: deal with them gently and take care lest we fall into the same entrapment of sin.[20]

[17] Eph. 5:3-7; Rom. 1:18-32
[18] Gal. 5:22-25
[19] Rom. 6:23
[20] Gal. 6:1

Judging in Review

1. Did you take time to check out the study texts?
   ___All ___Some ___None

2. As you judge your own life, would you say you have idols?
   Yes ___ No___

3. If yes, what are they? _____

4. Would you say that you tend to be critical and make judgements about your Christian brother or sister's walk with Christ?
   ___ Always ___Sometimes ___Never

5. I pride myself on being tolerant.
   ___Yes, Always ___ Sometimes ___Never

6. Do you read, understand and know The Bible?
   ___Yes ___ Some ___Not at all

7. Would you know if you or your Christian brother or sister were not living according to God's Word? ___Yes ___No ___ Maybe

8. Would you be comfortable speaking to a friend or acquaintance about a lifestyle contrary to God's Word?
   ___Yes, with God's help ___Maybe ___ No Absolutely

9. If you chose to speak, in what order would you do it? If there is anything you would not do, please cross it out; otherwise, list the order with #1 being the first thing to do:

   a. I would discuss with others to be sure they noticed the same thing(s) I did
   b. I would talk to the spouse or best friend to see if they would support my effort
   c. I would pray fervently to God about me
   d. I would pray fervently to God about the one caught in sin's snare

e. I would discuss this with the pastor

f. I would ask God to help me know what to say and how to say it

g. I would speak gently and lovingly, explaining my concern

SIN

Sin is the transgression of God's law.[1]

You might be thinking, but I thought Jesus did away with the law when He died on the cross. You are partially right. Jesus did do away with the Levitical law. This was a series of laws which encompassed the everyday occurrences in one's life. It covered food, clothing, pots and dishes, sickness, sexual relations and infection, as well as livestock, sacrifices, how to deal with neighbors and strangers and how to deal with infractions.[2]

The Old Covenant of the Levitical law was nailed to the cross when Jesus ushered in the New Covenant in His blood. Many guidelines of the Levitical code, however, are still useful today. As a matter-of-fact, many of our principles for infection control were first introduced by God through the Levitical code. Also, God-given guidelines for clean and unclean foods, when followed, still promote health.

Sin is the transgression of God's law as He gave it when He was here on earth. When He was asked to explain which commandment is the greatest commandment, He replied love the Lord God with all of your hearts, minds, and souls; and secondly, love your neighbor as yourself.[3] The first four of the Ten Commandments are summed up in the command to Love the Lord God with all of our hearts. The last six are summed up in the command to love our neighbor as ourselves. Jesus said, if we do these two things, we will fulfill the entire law. We are unable to do all of these things to perfection, because we are human. This is the law that God fulfilled for us when He died on the Cross. The fact that He fulfilled it doesn't mean that we no longer need to live by that law—it simply means that God's got our backs. By His sacrifice on the cross, He covers us.

Because we are human, we all sin[4] and God is compassionate and long-suffering with us because He knows we are just dust.[5] And so, we sin against God because we are imperfect. We sin against our family and our

---

[1] 1Jn. 3:4
[2] Lev. Chapters 11-15
[3] Mt. 22:37-39
[4] Rom. 3:23
[5] Gen. 2:7; 3:19

neighbors for the same reason. We are sinners. Sin separates us from our holy God and Jesus died to bridge that separation.

I have a friend who attends a church that proclaims unity. She thinks it's wonderful because they teach there is no such thing as sin. I wonder how they reconcile all of the horrible things that happen in this world, if there is no sin. But, really, her church is not alone. While many of the mainstream churches don't preach that there is no such thing as sin, they fail to preach about sin or call people to repentance. Attempting to be politically correct, preachers avoid the topic of sin so that no one will be offended. So, they go along, smiling, overlooking and many times condoning and participating in sin. The big problem is, by not addressing and condemning sin, they are actually leading people to hell. We have now come to an age where Christians live, dress and talk like the world.[6] God calls us to be salt and light to a world that is rushing to hell. As ambassadors for Christ, we need to be an example to the world of a new life in Christ.[7]

Jesus died for us so that we could leave our lives of sin. We don't have to be slaves to sin any longer. The Bible tells us that Jesus, because of the joy set before Him, endured the cross with its suffering and shame. The joy set before Him is the joy of having us love Him and be eager to go to Heaven with Him. Jesus is eager for a heart-relationship with us.[8]

Prior to Jesus' death on the cross, sin was often punished soon after it was committed. I think of 1. Nadab and Abihu, sons of Aaron, who played around at the altar by putting strange fire into their incense censers. Fire from the Lord devoured them.[9] 2. Achan, who stole plunder God said not to touch. Achan, his whole family and all of his flocks and herds were killed and then burned and buried.[10] 3. Hophni and Phineas, Eli's sons, belittled God's people and slept with the women who came to the temple. God allowed the Philistines to kill them.[11] Subsequently, every man in the family line died. 4. Ananias and Sapphira who lied to the Holy Ghost,

---

[6] Jas.4:4
[7] Ac. 5:20; Rom. 6:4
[8] Heb.12:2
[9] Lev. 10:1,2
[10] Jos. 7:3-26
[11] 1 Sam 2:12ff; 3:11-14

were killed immediately.[12] These are a few of those who suffered immediate punishment. God has not changed. His standards are still the same; but, final punishment will take place when He comes.

When Jesus died for our sins, He ushered in a time of grace. We are living under that grace at the present time. That means that, when we sin, we no longer immediately pay with our lives. Grace is God's unmerited favor—God does not treat us as our sins deserve.[13] We do, however, many times suffer the consequences of sin. For example, gluttony, substance abuse, unforgiveness, immorality and sexual perversion[14] all carry consequences.

The Unpardonable sin: Jesus told his disciples that there is a sin that cannot be forgiven. He said it is the sin against The Holy Ghost. This is the sin of which the religious leaders were guilty. They ascribed the workings of The Triune God to the devil.[15] The Holy Spirit calls the sinner to repentance and when that sinner repents, The Bible says there is great rejoicing in Heaven;[16] but sometimes the Holy Spirit works on one's heart for a long time only to be rebuffed. When He is continually, rebuffed, The Holy Spirit will no longer contend with man.[17] This is the unpardonable sin. That's why God says, "Today, if you hear the Holy Spirit's voice, don't harden your heart."[18]

Final Thoughts on Sin

Sin steals our peace and contentment. Sin kills our joy and the joy of those affected by our actions and destroys our lives here and for eternity. Thanks be to God, He provided a way for us to escape the clutches of sin. When we accept His sacrificial gift, He casts any remembrance of our sin into the deepest part of the sea. As far as the east is from the west, that is how far God has separated our sins from us.[19]

---

[12] Ac. 5::1-11
[13] Ps. 86:15; 103
[14] Rom.1:18ff
[15] Mt. 12:24; Mk 3:22
[16] Lk. 15:10
[17] Gen. 6:3; Ac. 24:24,27
[18] Heb. 3:12-15;4:7
[19] Ps. 103:12

Wide, wide as the ocean
High as the heavens above;
Deep, deep as the deepest sea
Is my Savior's love.
I, though so unworthy,
Still am a child of His care.
For His Word teaches me
That His love reaches me
Everywhere[20]

[20] Wide as the Ocean; C. Austin Miles, 1914

Sin Revisited

1. Did you take time to check out the study texts?
   ___ All ___ Some ___ None

2. Did you know there was a Levitical law? Yes___ No___

3. Did you know that Jesus ended the mandates of that law when He ushered in the New Covenant in His blood? Yes___ No___

4. Are you a sinner? Yes____ No___

5. Did you ever worry that you have committed the unpardonable sin? _____
   _____

6. Where are your sins, today? _____

DIET

A Lot of people in this world get really hung up on what other people are eating or drinking. The counsel given from God, through the Apostle Paul, is not to allow anyone to judge you in these matters.[1] As God's holy people, whatever we do should be done for His glory. He gives us these guideline:

1. Your body is the temple of God[2] and His Holy Spirit lives within you; therefore, whatever you put into it should honor God.

    We probably should consider cigarettes, alcohol, sugar in all forms, and every other substance that can be detrimental. Actually, even healthy substances, done to excess, can be harmful.

2. If you know that a Christian brother or sister would be offended by what you are eating or drinking, don't eat or drink it. Why risk causing your brother or sister to stumble?[3]

3. It would be better not to eat meat or drink wine or any other thing that would bring offense to your Christian family.[4]

4. Don't give a reason for people to look down on your faith, or on Jesus, because of something you choose to do.[5]

5. Whatever you think about disputable matters, keep it to yourself.[6]

6. If your Master is Jesus Christ, He will make you stand when all around you fall.[7]

The original diet that God gave man was every seed-bearing plant on the face of the whole earth and the fruit of every tree that had a seed in it.[8]

---

[1] Rom. 14
[2] 1Cor. 3:16,17
[3] Rom. 14:13-18
[4] Rom. 14:21
[5] Rom. 14: 22
[6] Rom. 14:22,23
[7] Rom. 14:3,4
[8] Gen.1:29

He specifically told them to eat from all of the fruit trees in The Garden of Eden, except the tree of the Knowledge of Good and Evil.

After the flood, which destroyed the whole earth, God told Noah, "Just as I previously gave you the green plants, now I give you everything. Everything that lives and moves will be food for you. BUT you must not eat meat that has its lifeblood still in it."[9] (In conjunction with this command, God said that anyone who sheds human blood should have his or her blood shed.) By adding meat to man's diet, God shortened mans' life. Prior to that event, man lived well into his hundreds. The oldest man was Methuselah, who lived to be 969 years old.

In the Book of Leviticus, God outlines what foods are clean and edible and what foods are unclean and are, therefore, not to be eaten. While the Levitical laws are no longer binding as a law of the land, there is wisdom in the directions given and they are beneficial to health.

Jesus told his followers that what goes into a person's mouth does not make him 'unclean;' but rather that which comes out of it. The first case may be a poor choice; but the latter is an indication of one's heart condition.

Final thoughts on Diet

Some have thought that Peter's vision of a sheet descending from heaven[10] has implications for our diet. The sheet had all manner of four-footed beasts and creeping things, snakes and birds in it and Peter was told, "Get up, Peter! Kill and eat." He received this vision three times and each time he responded in horror, "Certainly not, Lord! I've never eaten anything so gross"—actually he said impure and unclean. Each time, he heard God say, "Don't call anything impure or unclean that I have made clean." Immediately, there was a knock at the door and some men from the household of Cornelius, a Roman centurion, were standing there, asking Peter to accompany them to Cornelius' home. Immediately, God told Peter to go with them. The Jews at that time believed foreigners, such as these were impure and unclean.

[9] Gen. 9: 3-5
[10] Ac. 10:9-23;11:4-15

And, there you have it, that's the whole meaning of the vision—not permission to eat anything and everything, but a command to minister to people, even when they fall outside of our comfort zone.

Wisdom has built her house…
She has prepared her meat and mixed her wine.
She has set her table.
She calls from the highest point of the city:
"Let all who are simple come here!
"Leave your simple ways and you will live;
"Walk in the way of understanding…"
Instruct a wise man and he will be wiser still;
Teach a righteous man and he will add to his learning.
"The fear of the Lord is the beginning of wisdom,
And knowledge of the Holy One
Is understanding."[11]

[11] Prov. 9

Diet Revisited

1. Did you take time to check out the study texts?
___ All ___ Some ___ None

2. Did you know that God gave Adam and Eve the first Vegan diet?
Yes___ No___

3. Did you know that the addition of animal products occurred after the flood? Yes ___ No ___

4. Did you know that prior to the flood people lived well into their hundreds? (Methuselah lived to be 969) Yes___ No___

5. Were you aware that your Body is God's temple and His Holy Spirit resides in you? Yes ___ No___

6. What is your favorite thing to eat and or drink?_____

_____

7. Is that good for God's temple? Yes___ No___

8. Have you considered solemnly the things you put into your body? Yes___ No___

9. Is there anything about your diet that you want to change? Yes___ No___

What?_____

SALVATION
How can I know if I am saved

Some churches ignore the question of salvation, others teach that once you are saved you are always saved and still others say that when you die, you are maintained in a holding pattern while money is paid and prayers are said for your soul. How can we know who is right? How can we know what to believe?

I choose to study the Word of God and let it have the last and only Word on the subject.

What does God say?

Through the Apostle Paul God said, "If you confess with your mouth that Jesus is Lord and believe in your heart that God raised him from the dead, you will be saved. For it is with your heart that you believe and are justified and it is with your mouth that you confess and are saved."[1] You see, God doesn't say anything about any money being paid for the repose of your soul. After all, what can you purchase? God is the owner of everything and He, in the form of Jesus, died for your sins and mine. The debt is already paid—there is nothing you can add. It is as simple as that. When you are God's child, it's a done deal.

Jesus' blood, and your acceptance of that Gift, is the only transaction that matters to your salvation. As the hymn writer so beautifully said:

Jesus paid it ALL!
I Hear The Savior say,
"Thy strength indeed is small;
Child of weakness, watch and pray.
Find in Me thine all in all."
Jesus paid it all!
All to Him I owe.
Sin had left a crimson stain—
He washed it white as snow.[2]

[1] Rom. 10:9-11
[2] Jesus Paid it All; Elvira M. Hall 1854

What about once saved always saved?

It is true, that once you have sincerely asked Jesus to save you and to be Lord of your life, neither trouble, calamity, persecution, or danger can change Jesus' commitment to you. In the first place, you didn't choose Jesus—He chose you.[3] Oh, you probably said, "Jesus, I take you as my personal Savior, please save me" or something like that; but you wouldn't have sincerely said that if His Holy Spirit had not prompted you to say it.[4] Make no mistake, not everyone is God's child—only those He chose.[5]

Unfortunately, many who claim "once saved always saved" use their freedom in Christ to indulge their sinful nature.[6] This is not God's will. We are to work out our salvation with fear and trembling.[7] Yes, Jesus purchased our salvation but we have to work it out by making godly choices as to how to live our lives according to His Word.

The Bible is faithful when it tells us that neither life nor death nor principalities nor powers or anything in all creation can remove us from the love of God which is in Christ Jesus.[8] As children of God we can rest in full assurance that we are saved—God said so.

Can I Choose to Discard Salvation?

Absolutely we can discard salvation. Salvation is a gift that we must accept in order for it to become ours. By the same token, we can choose to play with it for a little while and then discard it. Have you ever given a gift to someone that wasn't accepted? Did you ever give a gift to someone who initially seemed pleased to receive it, but later you discovered it had been discarded?

Jesus said that He is not willing that any (of those whom He chose[9]) should perish.[10] He goes out on the highways and byways searching for

---

[3] Jn. 15:16
[4] Jn.6:44; 1Cor. 12:13; 2Tim. 1:14;
[5] Jn. 15:19; 17:6, 9,14,16,24-26; Rom. 9:6-24
[6] Gal. 5:13
[7] Php. 2:12,13
[8] Rom.8:38,39
[9] Jn. 17:9,24
[10] Mt. 18:14

His sheep and He rejoices, with the angels, when a sinner comes Home.[11] On the other hand, He will never force us to do what we don't want to do.

When Jesus told the parable of the farmer who went out to sow seed[12] He told about a group who received The Word with great gladness. The seed sown sprang right up! I've witnessed exactly that—perhaps you have, too. People become so thrilled with Jesus and immediately begin proclaiming their changed life; but they fail to get into The Word of God and pray. Before you know it, the plant begins to wither and die because it has no root! Interest is lost and they return to their old ways.

The writer of Hebrews wrote about this exact phenomenon.[13] Speaking through The Holy Spirit he said it is impossible for those once enlightened by The Gospel, who have tasted the Heavenly gift, shared in The Holy Spirit, tasted the goodness of The Word of God and the powers of the coming age, if they fall away, to be brought back to repentance; because, to their loss, their actions have crucified the Son of God all over again and subjected Him to public disgrace.

I don't believe God would have put that in The Bible if it wasn't possible for one who once professed Jesus Christ to walk away from Him and lose salvation.[14]

God counts us as watchmen to warn our Christian brothers and sisters when we see spiritual calamity coming or when we see them in sin. He specifically says that if we warn against these things we will possibly save the individuals' lives and we will definitely save ourselves. But, He says if we fail to give the warning, those sinning will die in their sins and we will be held accountable for their blood.[15] The watchman in Scripture was the prophet; but today, as ambassadors of Christ, we are all called to be watchmen.

---

[11] Lk. 15:4-7
[12] Mt. 13
[13] Heb. 6:4-6
[14] MK. 6:7 (read together) Jn. 18: 5,6 (Judas operated in gifts; Judas the betrayer)
[15] Ezk. 33

Final Thoughts on Salvation

When a sinner truly repents of sin, accepts God's free gift of Jesus' death to atone for that sin and asks Jesus to save him or her, Jesus freely gives salvation:

> For it is by grace you have been saved, through faith
> and that not of yourselves, it is the gift of God.
> Not by works,
> so that no one can boast.[16]
> If we confess our sins, He is faithful and just
> to forgive us our sins and
> cleanse us from all unrighteousness.[17]
> ...as far as the east is from the west,
> that is how far He has removed our transgressions from us.[18]

One can lose salvation by consciously choosing to walk away from loving Jesus and choosing instead to love the world.[19] Don't forget that Jesus said, "Not everyone who says to me, "Lord, Lord" will enter the Kingdom of Heaven; but only those who do the will of The Father."[20]

God does not arbitrarily kick anyone to the curb. His Holy Spirit woos the sinner to return; but there comes a time when He will no longer contend for the soul.[21] Rebuffing the Holy Spirit is the unpardonable sin.

We do not get to Heaven on our mother or father's shirttail. Each of us will stand, alone, before the judgement seat of Christ[22] to give an account of deeds done in the body, whether good or evil.[23] Be of good courage! God is Faithful. When we choose to abide in Him, He will cause our lives to be abundant in the fruits of His Spirit[24] and He will never leave us or forsake us.[25]

---

[16] Eph. 2:8
[17] 1Jn. 1:9
[18] Ps. 103:12
[19] 1Jn. 2:15-17
[20] Mt. 7:21
[21] Gen. 6:3; Mt. 12:31; Mk. 3:29
[22] 2Cor. 5:10
[23] Gal. 5:22-26
[24] Jn. 15:5
[25] Heb. 13:5

Amazing Grace, how sweet the sound
That saved a wretch like me.
I once was lost, but now am found;
Was blind, but now I see.
T'was Grace that caused my heart to fear
And Grace my fear relieved.
How precious did that Grace appear
The hour I first believed.
The Lord has promised good to me,
His Word my hope secures;
He will my Shield and Portion be,
As long as life endures.
Through many dangers, toils and strife
I have already come.
'Tis Grace that brought me safe thus far
And Grace will bring me Home!
When we've been there ten thousand years,
Bright shining as the sun,
We've no less days to sing God's praise
Than when we'd first begun.[26]

---

[26] Amazing Grace; John Newton, 1779

Salvation in Review

1. Did you take time to check out the study texts?
   ___All ___Some ___None

2. Have you taken inventory of your life to see how you stand before Christ? Yes___ No___

3. How did you do? _____

4. Are you working out your salvation with fear and trembling? Yes___ No___

5. How are you doing with that?_____

6. Can you say with confidence, "I am saved!"? Yes___ No___

7. Do you have Jesus' peace that surpasses earthly understanding? Yes___ No___

8. Have you assisted relatives or friends towards salvation? Yes___ No___

Are All Angels Holy?

No. All angels are not holy. God has thousands upon thousands of holy angels. He calls His angels "ministering spirits"[1] and says that they are sent to serve those who will inherit salvation. That's US! Who sends them? God sends them. We are not to pray to angels and we are not to go about seeking their involvement in our lives. We are to pray only to God in Jesus' Name. We can ask Him to send His angels and, as He sees fit, He will send them to minister to us. We never casually chat with angels; though, as God directs them, they will bring a message to us.

Seraphim (ser'$_e$-fim: Hebrew: saw-raf,[2] is derived from the root 'srp, which means to burn). Seraphim are fiery, burning angel-beings with six wings. In Scripture, the description is given that with two wings they fly, with two they cover their faces and with two they cover their feet.[3] They fly around the throne of God in Heaven singing praises and calling out His attributes:

"Holy, Holy, Holy is The Lord Almighty!
The whole earth is full of His glory!"[4]

Seraphim are instrumental in fiery judgements. The cities of Sodom and Gomorrah are examples of this fiery judgement. God rained down fire and brimstone on them. The judgement was that they were totally destroyed and would never rise again. This is an example of Hell Fire.[5]

When Isaiah began his ministry, he saw God on His throne and was so overwhelmed with his own unfitness to serve that he cried out, "Woe to me! I am ruined for I have unclean lips!" A seraph flew to him with a burning coal from Heaven's altar. To purify Isaiah for ministry, the seraph touched his lips with the live coal and told him his guilt was taken away and his sin had been atoned.

---

[1] Heb. 1:14
[2] Strong's Exhaustive Concordance on The Bible OT #8312
[3] Isa. 6:1-7
[4] Ibid
[5] Gen. 19:24; 2Pet. 2:6; Jude 7

We know that after Adam and Eve sinned they were expelled from The Garden of Eden. The Bible says, because they might have eaten from the Tree of Life and lived forever.[6] The angels sent to guard access to the tree were cherubim, the plural form of cherub. They were not babies with bow and arrow. They were mighty warrior angels having a flaming sword which flashed back and forth to guard the way to The Tree of Life and prevent entrance into the garden.

Carvings of cherubim covered the Mercy Seat on the Ark of the Covenant, and were prominent in the furnishings of the temple, which was designed by God.[7] The Bible says God sits enthroned between cherubim[8] and that, on occasion, God mounts the cherubim to fly—it must be great fun! Cherubim were instrumental in visions and messages to mankind.[9] The cherubim seen by Ezekiel had hands like a man, four faces and their wings were covered with eyes, denoting wisdom.

Lucifer (Satan) was the Guardian Cherub in Heaven, until his beauty puffed him up and he determined to become like God.[10] God booted him off the mount of God and he's been doing his best to corrupt mankind with malice, envy, strife, greed, bloodshed and every other sin ever since. Some of what God says about Satan has happened and some is yet to come. Prophecy is like that, appearing immediate, appearing near and appearing far (kind of like mountains we view when driving across country).

The Bible says there was war in Heaven. Michael, the archangel,[11] and his angels fought against the dragon and the dragon's angels. The dragon and his angels fought back, but could not prevail against Michael and the holy angels. The dragon and his angels lost their place in Heaven. The Bible indicates that the dragon swept one-third of the angels (stars) out of Heaven with him.[12] The devil and his angels were hurled down—I love that phrase "hurled down"! It speaks of drama and the victory, which we will

---

[6] Gen. 3:22,24
[7] Ex. 25;26;36;37
[8] Ps. 18:10; 80:1; Isa. 37:16
[9] Ezk. 10:9-17
[10] Ezk.. 28:11-19 KIV (The King of Tyre is an analogy of Satan); Isa.14:12-20
[11] Rev. 12:7-9; Dan. 10:13,21(angel Michael battled Satan to assist the answer to Daniel's prayer) ; 12:1(angel Michael protects God's people); Jude 9 (angel Michael battled Satan over Moses' body)
[12] Rev. 12:9

eventually realize in Jesus. Jesus told His disciples, "I saw Satan fall like lightening from Heaven."[13]

Many people today are fooled by demonic angels who masquerade as servants of righteousness.[14] We have "Christians" today who are calling psychic hot-lines, conversing with unholy angels, watching and participating in programs where loved ones are supposedly channeled, playing with Ouija boards, having tarot cards and tea leaves read, following horoscopes, practicing Yoga, playing demonic computer games, reading and watching horror stories and paranormal thrillers. "Christians" are participating in sexual liaisons, pornography, orgies and other activities that God says will result in eternal death.[15] So many Christians are ignorant of God's Word! God says that all such things have their origin in Satan[16] and are sinful, blasphemous activities—the end thereof is eternal death.

You'll notice as you read these texts that God includes among these sins, making one's son or daughter pass through the fire. This is a grievous sin which has been being perpetrated by Satan for thousands of years! In the past, parents sacrificed their children to the detestable heathen gods, Moloch and Baal.[17] God said He would never have even considered asking His people to do such a terrible thing. We are ignorant of the fact that it is God who opens a mother's womb,[18] enabling her to have the gift of children. Today, we thoughtlessly cause our children to "pass through the fire" when we destroy them in the mother's womb. We burn the children to death with high concentrate saline, which is extremely caustic. We practice and condone partial birth abortion; in which the baby's head is delivered. Then the doctor sticks a forceps or scissors into the brain stem—the baby screams in pain. This sacrifice is made to the god of convenience. God can and will forgive this terrible sin, if we sincerely repent; but, those who remain unrepentant will forfeit eternal life when they stand before God at the judgement.[19]

---

[13] Lk. 10:18
[14] 2Cor. 11:14,15
[15] Lev..18:22-25; Rom. 1:18-32
[16] Lev..19:31;20:6;Deut.18:10-12;2Ki.16:3;17:16,17;21;Isa.8:19,20;19:2-4;Jer.32:35;
[17] Lev. 18:2; Ps. 106:37; Jer. 19:5
[18] Ps. 139 13; 1Sam. 1:5,6,17-20; 2Sam. 6:16,20-23; Isa. 44:2,24; Jer. 1:5 (The Lord creates inside a mother's womb; He opens or closes it)
[19] Mt. 7:21-23;2Cor. 5:10

Final Thoughts on Angels, Demons, the Occult

Don't let anyone take your crown.[20]

While you are taking your spiritual inventory, check out how you measure up in the witchcraft, tarot cards, occult inspired activities, books, movies and horoscope department. How about occult inspired dolls and comics? These activities leave us open to demonic influences which can bring on demonic attacks of depression, other illness and suicide.

People frequently ask if Christians can be attacked by Satan.[21] The answer is, yes, faithful Christians can be attacked. We need only look at the lives of Adam and Eve,[22] Abel,[23] Job,[24] Joseph,[25] Daniel,[26] James, Peter,[27] Paul,[28] John,[29] each of the other disciples and Jesus to see that Satan was allowed to have his way with them for a certain amount time.

Actually, everyone in Scripture who followed Our Lord came under Satan's attack. Everyone who faithfully follows Jesus today will, as well, come under the attack of Satan.[30] In each case, Satan was, and is, allowed to have his way for a time. The Bible tells us that a curse can be attempted against us; but a curse that is undeserved will not remain.[31]

You can read further in The Bible about instances of visitations by holy angels. Check out the stories of Abraham,[32] Jacob,[33] Samson,[34] Daniel,[35] the birth of John the Baptist,[36] the birth of Jesus[37] and many more.

---

[20] Rev.3:11
[21] Job 1:1-42:17
[22] Gen. 3:1-19;4:8-12
[23] Gen. 4:8
[24] Job 1:1-12; 2:1-6
[25] Gen.37:3-28; 39:1-2,23;40:1-23
[26] Dan. 6
[27] Lk. 22:31 Ac. 12: 1-19; .
[28] Ac.16-31; 21:27-36; 23:12-22
[29] Rev. 1:9 (John was imprisoned on Patmos)
[30] Mt. 5:10-12; 10:21,22; Jn. 17:14,15; 2Tim. 3:12
[31] Prov. 26:2
[32] Gen. 18:1-15
[33] Gen. 28:10ff
[34] Jdg. 13:2-21
[35] Dan.10:4-21ff
[36] Lk. 1:5-25;57-66
[37] Mt. 1:18-21; Lk.1:26-38; 2:6--14

Angels, Demons and the Occult in review

1. Did you take time to check out the study texts?
___All ___Some ___None

2. Had you ever heard of Seraphim? Yes___ No___

3. Did you know that the name Seraphim denotes fire?_____

4. Were you surprised to know that Seraphim are fervent in worship and praise and have participation in fiery judgement of people and cities? Yes___ No___

5. Were you surprised to learn that Cherubs and Cherubim are not fat babies with bows and arrows? Yes___ No___

6. Did you know that God has so much to say against involvement in the occult on all levels? Yes___ No___

7. Have you participated in any of these practices? Yes___ No___

8. If yes, are you ready to get on your knees today and repent and ask God to forgive you? Yes___ No___

9. Have you ever before considered that Christians might be attacked by demonic spirits? Yes___ No___

THE SACRAMENTS
MARRIAGE
Instituted by God in the Garden of Eden[1]

On the sixth literal day of creation, God said, referring to His triune qualities, "Let us make man in our image."[2] God formed man and woman from the dust of the ground and called them "man." Adam was formed first and God breathed into his nostrils the breath of life and man became a living soul. God put Adam into the beautiful Garden of Eden to tend it. One wonders what there was that needed tending, since dew from the ground watered the earth, nothing died and there were no thorns or weeds. Perhaps Adam's job was to pet and cuddle the animals and play with the fish, since none was fearful of him.

The Bible says that in the cool of the day, The Lord God walked in The Garden and I am sure the man walked with Him.

God wanted Adam to have a companion because, He said, "It is not good for the man to be alone…I am going to make him a suitable helper!"[3] In preparation for this special creation event, God caused all of the animals and birds that He had created to pass before Adam to see what he would call each one.[4] It must have been a wonderful time as Adam saw each beautiful creature for the first time and called its name. I envision both God and Adam laughing with joy and delight as Adam discovered the antics of each animal and bird and marveled at the myriad of colors God had created.[5] As the animals passed before him, Adam must have noted that each one had a similar but different mate—but he did not. He must have wondered why there was no partner that resembled him.

God, the Master Physician, administered the first ever anesthesia and performed the first surgery! God caused Adam to fall into a deep sleep. Adam was sound asleep when God took a rib from under his arm and then closed the place with flesh. Around that rib, God fashioned a woman from the dust of the ground and brought her to Adam. Imagine his surprise and

---

[1] Gen. 2:18,21-25
[2] Gen. 1:26
[3] Gen,2:18
[4] Ps. 139:4 (God knows every word before it leaves our lips; who actually named he animals?)
[5] Heb. 1:8-12 (note the name of the Creator); Gen. 1:31; 2:1

delight, upon waking, to see such a beautiful friend! Here was the creature that resembled him! With joy, Adam announce, "This is bone of my bone and flesh of my flesh! I will call her 'woman' because she was taken out of man."[6] Adam and his wife were naked and they were not ashamed.

For this reason, man is to leave his father and mother and be united to his wife, and they will become one flesh.[7]

Notice that God did not form the woman from Adam's head so she would rule over and control him; nor did He form her from Adam's foot so that he could mistreat and abuse her. God formed woman from a rib taken from under Adam's arm, close to is heart, so that he would see her as his equal helper and would honor her, love and protect her.

God performed the first marriage ceremony right there in The Garden of Eden. He instructed the man and woman on how to care for one another, love each other, produce children and play together.

God commanded that the marriage bed is to be honored by all and kept pure; for God will judge the adulterer and all the sexually immoral.[8]

> God made man in his own image,
> in the image of God He created him;
> male and female He created them.
> God blessed them and said to them,
> "Be fruitful and increase in number;
> fill the earth and subdue it.
> Rule over the fish of the sea, the birds of the air
> and over every living creature on the ground.
> Then He gave them a diet of every seed-bearing plant
> on the face of the whole earth
> and every tree that bears fruit with a seed in it.[9]

---

[6] Gen. 2:23
[7] Gen. 2:24,25
[8] Heb. 13:4; Rom.1:18-32
[9] Gen 1:27-29

Adam named his wife "Eve" because she would become the mother of all living.[10] From this one man came every nation of men so that they would inhabit the whole earth.[11]

It was God's plan that husbands and wives should have loving tender relationships because He uses the marriage relationship to help us understand His own relationship to His church. Jesus is the Bridegroom. The Church is the Bride of Christ.

God tells us, through the Apostle Peter, that the husband is to submit himself to The Lordship of Jesus Christ and is to love his wife just as Christ loves the church, even being willing to give his life to protect her. The husband is to love his wife even as he loves his own body and not hurt or misuse her. God cautions the husband to be very careful how he treats his wife; because being harsh or unkind will prevent his prayers from being heard or answered.[12]

Women are to be submissive to their own husbands; for, just as Christ is The Head of His church, so the husband is the head of the husband-wife relationship. When a wife is loved as outlined by God, it is an easy thing to submit to her loving husband. When the husband loves his wife as God loves His church, he thinks of her needs before even she does.

God wants the husband and wife relationship to be fun and fulfilling. Husbands and wives are to fulfill their marital duty and not withhold themselves from each other. The husband and wife are one; therefore, their bodies belong to each other. It is God's will that they enjoy intimate pleasure with each other and only abstain from sexual relations by mutual consent, for a short period of time, in order to devote oneself to special prayer. An example would be for a brief, agreed upon time, of fasting. Once this brief time is complete, they must come together again to continue their intimate love life. In this way neither party will be tempted by Satan to stray from the marriage bed.[13] When a Holy Spirit-filled husband and wife come together in intimate union, tensions are relieved, relationships are renewed and there is joy in meeting one another's needs.

---

[10] Gen. 3:20
[11] Ac. 17:26
[12] 1Pet. 3:7; Eph.5: 25-33
[13] 1 Cor.7:3-5

Marriage should never be entered into lightly—it is a lifetime commitment. God hates divorce.[14] When a couple enters into marriage, it would be well to mutually agree never to use the term "divorce" in reference to one's own marriage. The devil is out to steal, kill and destroy marriages and families. We must make a conscious effort to safeguard our relationships.

God cautions us not to allow the sun to go down while we are angry[15] because anger does not bring about the righteous life God desires.[16] Make up your mind to always make up before going to sleep—it's healthy for your relationship and it is fun! The couple, who prays together, stays together; so, in this way, make every effort to let the peace of God rule in your hearts.[17]

Final Thoughts on Marriage

Thou shalt not commit adultery.[18] God told us to leave father and mother and all that would separate us and *cling* to each other. Adultery is destructive to the marital union because it breaks trust, destroys self and belittles the relationship. It is destructive to the guilty party because it erodes the steadfast heart and mind.

The Bible says that we are to flee sexual immorality. Every other sin we commit is outside of the body; but, those who sin sexually, sin against their own bodies. We who have united with The Lord have His spirit living within us. We were bought with a price—we must not allow sin to reign in these Temples of the Holy Spirit.[19]

The devil is no respecter of persons, so I address both men and women as I caution you about his wiles. He tempts both men and women to pursue destructive activity. We may destroy our marriage by giving our male and female friends priority over our spouses. God tells us to forsake all others.

---

[14] Mal. 2:16
[15] Eph. 4:26
[16] Jas. 1:20
[17] Php. 4:7
[18] Ex. 20:14; Mt, 19:18
[19] 1Cor. 6:18-20

The Bible speaks against the lust of the eyes, looking with lustful thoughts at a man or a woman.[20] God's servant, Job said he made a covenant with his eyes not to look lustfully at a girl.[21] Today we have to include both marriage partners who need to guard against looking lustfully at anyone, male or female. We may not go bed hopping, but God says if we look with lust at anyone, we have committed adultery in our hearts.[22] Pornography can be a challenge because it breaks onto computers, without invitation—that's how sneaky the devil is. Pornography and suggestive content is in advertisements, catalogs and salacious conversation. It is rarely possible to see a movie without being subjected to Satan's agenda via previews, if not in the movie itself. The devil has no end of ways to snare the careless Christian. He is full of fury because he knows his time is short.[23] Therefore, we must guard the avenues of the soul: eyes, ears, taste, smell and touch. Keep your eyes on Jesus!

He, who pursues righteousness and love,
finds life, prosperity and honor.[24]

O, Perfect Love
All human thought transcending
Lowly we kneel in prayer before Thy throne.
That theirs may be a love that knows no ending
Whom Thou forevermore does join in one.
O, perfect life
Be thou their full assurance
Of tender charity and steadfast faith;
Of patient hope and quiet, brave endurance,
With childlike trust that fears not pain nor death.
Grant them the joy which brightens earthly sorrow;
Grant them the peace which calms all earthly strife.
Add to life's day the glorious unknown morrow
That dawns upon eternal love and life.[25]

---

[20] 1Jn. 2:16
[21] Job 31:1
[22] Mt. 5:28
[23] Rev. 12:12Lp
[24] Prov. 21:21
[25] O Perfect Love; Dorothy Blomfield Gurney; 1858

Marriage in Review

1. Did you take time to check out the study texts?
   ___All ___Some ___None

2. Did you know that God invented marriage to be between one man and one woman? Yes___ No___

3. Did you know that God commanded that neither husband nor wife should put others before their spouse? Yes___ No___

4. Do you know that over-involvement in good things (e.g. church) can be detrimental to your marital relationship? Yes___ No___

5. Were you surprised to know that God gave the first instruction on health & sexuality? Yes___ No___

6. Did you know that, as The Master Physician, God administered the first anesthetic and performed the first surgery? Yes___ No___

7. Were you surprised to know that God wants married couples to enjoy sex? Yes___ No___

8. If you are married, did you make a lifetime commitment to your spouse? Yes___ No___

Baptism

There are many baptisms spoken of in The Bible; but, the baptism that makes all of the difference to us, as we contemplate discipleship, is the baptism of Jesus by his cousin, John.[1]

John came baptizing in the desert region and preaching a baptism of repentance for the forgiveness of sins. The whole Judean countryside and all the people of Jerusalem went out to him. Confessing their sins, they were baptized by John in the Jordan River.[2]

The Pharisees had invented various ceremonial washings as an outward sign to others of their holiness. Jesus did not present Himself to the religious leaders at the temple in Jerusalem. Instead, He presented Himself to John, in the wilderness, to be baptized in the Jordan. By coming to John, Jesus was commending to the people John's ministry and saying, in effect, "Listen to John and obey him." Instead, the religious leaders chose to reject John's ministry.

John was surprised that Jesus would come to him to be baptized and objected saying, "I need to be baptized by you!" Jesus replied, "Let it be so now, to fulfill all righteousness." In being baptized by John, Jesus fulfilled the priestly washings prescribed under the Old Testament priesthood.[3] God had instructed that the priest was to be consecrated through washing and then be anointed with oil, representing the Holy Spirit.[4] Jesus was baptized by immersion in the Jordan and then The Holy Spirit descended upon Him, as a dove.[5]

John, who was Jesus' cousin, was six months older than Jesus and began his ministry about six months prior to Jesus coming to him to be baptized. John was approximately half-way through his ministry at that time. Herod the Tetrarch had John beheaded about six months later.

---

[1] Lk. 1 (esp. v.36,56)
[2] Mk. 1:4,5
[3] Ex.30:17-21,30-33
[4] Oil represents the Holy Spirit; Ex. 29:7; 1Sam. 10:1; Ps.23:5; 89:20; 133:1-3;Mt.25:1-13(esp.7-10,12,13);Jas. 5:13-16
[5] Mt. 3:16,17

Jesus continued the ministry of John's baptism; although it was not Jesus doing the baptizing, but His disciples.[6] The disciples continued the ministry of baptism after Jesus returned to Heaven. The Book of Acts gives the account of the early church, known as "The Way," and of the new converts confessing their sins and being baptized by immersion.

Today, we have many churches which have chosen to follow a more convenient way of sprinkling or pouring. Jesus' command was "Go and teach all nations, baptizing them in the Name of The Father, The Son and The Holy Ghost."[7] The Apostle Peter said, "Repent_and be baptized every one of you for the forgiveness of your sins and you will receive the gift of the Holy Spirit."[8] The message was: The Gospel and repentance. Those who accepted the message repented and were baptized. The Bible records that about three thousand were added to their number in ONE day.[9] That must have been some baptism!

Jesus' example was that of baptism by immersion. Immersion is significant. The Apostle Paul says we are, therefore, buried with Christ in baptism into death in order that, just as Christ rose from the dead through the glory of The Father, so we, too, may walk in newness of life.[10]

The Apostle Peter, further, likens Noah's ark carrying eight people to safety through the flood waters as symbolizing baptism that now saves us—not by the removal of dirt from the body; but by the pledge of a good conscience toward God. It saves us by the resurrection of Jesus Christ.[11]

The important thing in baptism is to believe that Jesus is the Son of God, repent of one's sins and be baptized with water.[12]

The Apostle Paul (Saul) was a very zealous Jew, a Pharisee, who persecuted and killed followers of The Way; but, then Jesus confronted him on the road to Damascus. Saul was going to Damascus with letters from the high priest

---

[6] Jn. 4:1,2
[7] Mt.28:19
[8] Ac. 2:38
[9] Ac. 2:41
[10] Rom. 6:4
[11] 1 Pet. 3:20-21
[12] Ac. 16:31-33

giving him permission to drag Christians from their homes to persecute and kill them. After his encounter on the Damascus road, he professed his belief on Jesus, repented of his sins and immediately was baptized. His name was changed to Paul.

Final Thoughts on Baptism

The thief, who accepted Jesus as His Savior while hanging on the cross,[13] is an example of one who was promised Heaven without being baptized. I believe God graciously added that story in Scripture to encourage those who desire to follow Jesus but are unable to be baptized due to reasons which include infirmity or incarceration. We are saved by accepting Jesus' death on the cross and repenting of our sins.

Infant baptism began during Baal worship; but entered the Christian church about the third century (Council of Carthage 416A.D.) not long after Emperor Constantine (272 A.D.- 337 A.D.). While Constantine outwardly professed Christianity, he continued to venerate the sun and participate in pagan sacrifice. He considered himself Christ-like and his mausoleum shows him as Christ, surrounded by twelve monuments, each containing, what was said to be, relics of an apostle. Constantine was baptized on his death bed, by a Catholic priest. Out of this baptized paganism came, among other things, infant baptism. Parents who refused to baptize their infants were labeled "Anabaptists" and were persecuted and killed.[14]

Some churches continue to practice infant baptism. Infant baptism, in the Christian church, is really nothing more than parents taking their little ones to the pastor or priest to dedicate them to God. Jesus' parents took Him to the temple when he was eight days old, to present Him to the priest. When parents dedicate their baby they—not the baby—are making a promise. They are promising, before God, to raise their child to follow Jesus Christ, according to the precepts of The Bible.

I wonder how many parents understand this solemn event; or do they just see this as a time of ceremony, celebration and a cause for picture taking?

---

[13] Lk. 23:32-43
[14] The Trail of Blood; James Milton Carroll,1852-1931

I wonder... There is no repentance, no profession of belief in Jesus because the baby is incapable of such comprehension. Parents cannot believe or repent for their child.

Why do parents seek infant baptism for their children? Are they afraid that if the child dies they will not go to Heaven? Well, infant baptism is not going to get them to Heaven. Children who die prior to the age of accountability belong to God. The infant goes directly to be with God.[15] Older children are judged by their hearts, which parents shape for Jesus—or not. This is why understanding infant dedication is so important. Jesus loves the little children and loves to have them come to Him.[16] Don't you know that you can trust Jesus to keep your child, without resorting to pagan hocus pocus? Don't you know that if God required infant baptism in order for a child to go Heaven, Jesus would have told us?

Hopefully, the parents of baptized infants and children will tell the child often of the dedication and the promise they made to teach the child to follow Jesus. Hopefully, they will assist that child to follow Jesus' plan for his or her life. Their child's future commitment to Jesus depends upon what the parents and the church teach. If the child is taught well, then, as he or she gets older, the promises made by their parents will become their own. It would be tragic for parents to teach their children that because they were baptized as an infant they are sure to go to Heaven. Going to Heaven requires acknowledging sin, repenting of it and making a personal choice to live for Jesus. I didn't say that, God did.

Most churches that practice infant baptism have confirmation classes. In this rite, the child confirms that they believe church teachings and is admitted to membership in the church. Hopefully, the child recognizes sin in his or her life. At that point they must express a belief in Jesus and repent of any sins they recognize and pledge to live for Jesus. This can happen when the child is old enough to understand sin and repentance and understand that Jesus' death on the cross was for them. My prayer is that they will choose, at that point, to be baptized.

---

[15] Job 3:10-18; 10):18,(Job was speaking prior to Jesus' death
[16] Mt. 19:14

Baptism Revisited

1. Did you take time to check out the study texts?
___All ___Some ___None

2. When Jesus was baptized, did you realize that He was fulfilling Old Testament priestly requirements? Yes___ No___

3. Were you surprised to know that Jesus modeled baptism by immersion and that all converts in the early church were baptized by immersion? Yes___ No___

4. Were you aware that infant baptism is never spoken of nor practiced in Scripture? Yes___ No___

5. Does knowing that, and its history, bother you? Yes___ No___

6. Are you troubled by the practice of infant baptism in your church? Yes___ No___

SERVANTHOOD
Ordinance of Humility / Foot Washing

One day, the mother of James and John approached Jesus to request that, when His kingdom was established, her sons would be seated, one on His right and one on His left.

When the other disciples learned of this they were indignant! So, Jesus called them all together and reminded them of how Gentile rulers lord it over them and how the Jewish officials were in authority over them. He told them,

> "This is not what I want from you.
> If you believe you are great, then first choose to be a servant to all.
> I, The Son of Man, did not come to be served,
> I came to serve and to give My life as a ransom for many."[1]

***

When Jesus went up to Jerusalem to celebrate The Passover, His disciples prepared the room and when the appointed time came, they all went in and reclined at table.

The food was being served, when Jesus arose from His place, left the meal and removed His outer clothing. He wrapped a towel around His waist, poured water into a basin and began to wash His disciples' feet, drying them with the towel around His waist.[2]

When Jesus came to Simon Peter, Peter was incredulous.

"Lord, are you going to wash *my* feet?!" he exclaimed.

Jesus replied, you do not understand now what I am doing for you; but one day you will."

Like John, when Jesus came to him for baptism, Peter felt unworthy.

---

[1] Mt. 20:21-28; Mk. 10:37-45
[2] Jn. 13:2-5

"No, Lord," he said. "You are never going to wash my feet!"

Jesus explained, "Peter, if I do not wash your feet, you have no part with Me."

"Well, In that case," acquiesced Peter, "don't just wash my feet, wash my head and hands, too!"

When Jesus was done washing the disciples' feet, He removed the towel and replaced His outer garments. Then He returned to His place at table.[3]

Jesus washing Peter's feet

---

[3] Jn. 13:4-12,34-35;1Pet. 5:6,7

"Do you understand what I have done for you?" Jesus asked.

"You call me Teacher and Lord—and you should because that is who I am. Now that I, your Lord and Teacher have washed your feet, you also should wash one another's feet. I have set for you an example. You should do what I have done for you.[4]

> No servant is greater than his Master,
> No messenger is greater than The One who sent him.
> Now that you know these things,
> You will be blessed if you do them.[5]

Jesus is our example. He told His disciples, "Now that I, your Lord and Teacher have washed your feet, you also should wash one another's feet. I have set an example that you should do as I have done for you."

> When Jesus died upon Calvary's tree
> He gave His life that I might be free.
> Serving Him daily, forsaking the past,
> I would be like Him while life here shall last.
> More like the Master In word and thought and deed.
> More like the Master, humbly I plead.
> Wherever I go, where're I may be
> Master, make me more like Thee.[6]

---

[4] Jn. 13:12-15
[5] Jn. 13:16,17
[6] More Like Thee O Master; Curtis B. Davis; 1946

Servanthood in Review

1. Did you take time to check out the study texts?
   ___All ___Some ___None

2. Have you ever before considered the implications of Jesus washing His disciples' feet? Yes___ No___

3. Do you believe it is an important message? Yes___ No___

4. Have you ever participated in a foot washing celebration? Yes___ No___

5. Would you like to? Yes___ No___

6. Would you feel comfortable suggesting it to a group of your friends? Yes___ No___

7. Could you relate to your friends what Jesus did for His disciples? Yes___ No___

8. Do you think the faith community would benefit from this in a discussion of servanthood? Yes ___ No___

THE LORD'S SUPPER
Eucharist / Communion

Just prior to going to the cross, Jesus had a last supper with His disciples. So, for purposes of this study, we will choose to call it, The Last Supper.

Every time God has introduced a major event, He has created a memorial so we will remember. His memorials are to be shared with friends and family, so that we will never forget what God did. The Last Supper was taken from the Passover meal so, it seems appropriate to have an understanding about that institution.

God's children were slaves in Egypt for four-hundred years. Their work was hard and their taskmasters were cruel. The people cried and cried and cried out to God and He heard them crying. The Bible says that He saw the Israelites and He was concerned about them[1] and He chose Moses to assist in rescuing them. God confronted Moses from a burning bush on Mount Horeb, the Mountain of God. Moses went over to see a strange sight: a bush on fire but not being consumed! God called to him from out of the bush, "Take off your shoes, Moses, because the ground on which you are standing is holy." Then, God told him, "I have seen the misery of my people in Egypt. I have heard them crying out because of their slave drivers, and I am concerned about their suffering…" He told Moses He had chosen him to assist in bringing about His children's deliverance. You can read the story in the Book of Exodus.[2]

During the course of deliverance, God brought ten plagues upon Egypt because their ruler, Pharaoh, had a stubborn heart. He refused to let God's people go. The final plague, which brought about Israel's deliverance, was that of the death angel passing over all the homes in Egypt. At midnight, every firstborn son of both man and beast was killed.[3]

In preparation for that plague, God gave instructions in order to preserve His chosen people. He instructed Moses to tell every family to kill a lamb and sprinkle its blood on the frames and tops of the doors of their homes

---
[1] Ex. 2:25
[2] Ex. 1;2;3
[3] Ex.12; Isa. 13:11; Dan. 4:37 (God knows how to humble the proud)

and barns. When the angel of death saw the blood, he would pass over their homes and their firstborn would be spared.

That same night they were to roast the lamb[4] over a fire and eat it with bitter herbs[5] and bread without yeast.[6] They were to eat it with their cloaks tucked into their belts, sandals on their feet and their staves in their hands. They were to eat it in haste and any lamb leftover was to be burned immediately. This was The Lord's Passover to commemorate, for His people, their deliverance from slavery.[7]

Now, when Jesus, The Lamb of God, was about to deliver His people from slavery to sin and Satan, He instituted The Last Supper with His Disciples. It took place in Jerusalem, at Passover, on the Day of the feast of Unleavened Bread.

Jesus told His disciples:
I have eagerly desired to eat this Passover with you
before I suffer.
I will never eat it again
until it finds fulfillment
in the Kingdom of God.[8]

On the first day of the Feast of Unleavened Bread the Passover
Lamb, a lamb without blemish[9], was to be slaughtered.[10]

The basic Passover meal:
Lamb
Bitter greens
Salt water
Unleavened Bread
Four cups of red wine

---

[4] A fore-symbol of the Lamb of God
[5] Representing bitter years of slavery
[6] Representing freedom from sin
[7] Ex. 12:3-11
[8] Lk. 22:15,16
[9] Represents Jesus Christ, the spotless Lamb of God
[10] Mk. 14:12

In the Jewish home, a careful search is done, prior to Passover; to be sure there is not a speck of yeast within the house.[11] The lamb[12] is roasted and eaten with bitter herbs[13] which are dipped in salt water.[14] This is eaten with unleavened bread.[15] There are four cups of red wine: representing Sanctification/Salvation; Judgment/Plagues; Redemption/Blessing; Acceptance/Praise.[16]

Jesus took the first cup, representing sanctification and salvation, and gave thanks. Then He gave it to His disciples saying,

> Take this and divide it among you.
> For I tell you,
> I will not drink of
> The fruit of the vine again until the
> Kingdom of God comes.[17]

The unleavened bread is broken into three pieces. The third part is hidden from view (as though buried). At the end of the meal, the youngest person present—usually a child—is sent to find the hidden bread and bring it out. That bread is then broken and distributed among the dinner guests. This is the bread which Jesus distributed among His disciples saying, "Take, eat; this is my body broken for you; do this in remembrance of Me."[18]

God's supernatural hand definitely was in the formation of the Passover.

Then Jesus took the bread and broke it saying,

> This is my body, broken for you;
> Do this in remembrance of Me.[19]

---

[11] Yeast represents sin
[12] Represents Jesus Christ, the spotless Lamb of God
[13] Represents the cruelty of bondage and slavery
[14] Represents the tears shed during Egyptian slavery
[15] Represents Jesus, the sinless Bread of Life
[16] Four cups of Passover; Jews for Jesus
[17] Lk. 22:17
[18] Jews for Jesus.org
[19] Lk. 22:19

After supper, He took the third cup, the cup representing redemption and blessing and gave thanks saying,

> This is The New Covenant
> in My blood,
> Which is poured out for many,
> for the forgiveness of sins.
> I tell you,
> I will not drink of this fruit of the vine
> From now on until that day
> When I drink it anew in The Kingdom of God.[20]

This is God's memorial of Jesus' death on the cross to free us from the slavery of our sins. This memorial is His promise of salvation. He tells us, as often as we take this cup, we are to do it in remembrance of Him.

The counsel of God, through the Apostle Paul, is that when we take the bread or drink the cup of The Lord we must ensure that we are standing in right relationship before Him—to be sure we are not drinking of it unworthily. Participating in factions, divisions, immorality, living in sin or unforgiveness will bring judgement from The Lord; because we are sinning against God. To partake carelessly, without realizing that the emblems symbolize The Lord's body, is eating and drinking judgement upon ourselves. For this reason, many are weak and sick or have died. Paul recommends we judge ourselves, so that we don't come under the judgement of The Lord.[21]

Final Thoughts on the Last Supper

Jesus set prescribed guideline for partaking of the Last Supper.

Jesus never said
1. That the bread and wine undergo some mysterious transubstantiation into His actual body and blood. No, He was sitting right there with His disciples when He said, "This is My body"…"This

---

[20] Mk. 14:24,25
[21] 1Cor. 11:17-34

is My blood." He very clearly indicated these are *symbols* of His body and blood.

Jesus did say

2. To the people following after Him, "I tell you the truth, unless you eat the flesh of the Son of Man and drink His blood, you have no life in you. Whoever eats my flesh and drinks my blood has eternal life and I will raise him up at the last day."[22] After hearing Jesus say that, many followers deserted Him (many followed just to see miracles).

Jesus was not referring to cannibalism. He was speaking to the intensity of their belief and their decision to follow Him. A true disciple of Christ will follow Jesus wherever He goes, even to martyrdom, if necessary. A true disciple does not just trot along to see miracles and find something to chat about. Jesus' life actually becomes a living, vital part of the lives of His true followers.

Jesus never said

3. Only priests, pastors or others deemed appropriately holy are to serve the Last Supper.

Of course it is appropriate that it be shared in a worship setting; but Jesus' intention was that friends and families would share it together and *remember* and talk about His sacrificial gift. Families should share this memorial and talk about the holiness of the God who instituted it and the meaning and significance of His death on the cross. It is appropriately shared in intimate settings between husband and wife, with the family and with friends.

In our churches, it has often spiraled-down to just another thing we do at specific times throughout the year. It has become rote. People, and many times children, are simply going through the motions of something we do. The memorial has lost its meaning.

---

[22] Jn. 6:50ff

I once heard a group, together with their pastor, laughing about hiding Easter eggs[23] on the communion table. Sadly, there is often no distinction made between things holy and things profane. God killed Nadab and Abihu for that lack of distinction.[24]

Jesus did say

4. I will never again drink of the fruit of the vine until that day when I take it with you in The Kingdom. That is why He refused the wine-vinegar offered to Him as He hung on the cross. Jesus is a covenant-keeping God.

Take of the Bread and the Wine,

Do it often.

In remembrance of Me.[25]

Until it is fulfilled in the Kingdom of God.

---

[23] goddessgift.org;Babylonia,fertility goddess Ishtar, decorated eggs
[24] Lev. 10:1,2
[25] Lk. 22:19; 1Cor. 11:24-26

The Lord's Supper Revisited

1. Did you take time to check out the study texts?
    ___All ___Some ___None

2. Did you know that Jesus was bringing the old covenant, with all of its Levitical rules and regulations, to an end and instituting a new covenant ushering in Grace? Yes___ No___

3. Have you been in the habit of partaking of the Lord's Supper carelessly, because it's just another thing you always do at church? Yes___ No___

4. Are you often moved to tears when you contemplate the sacrifice of God on your behalf? Often___ Never___

5. Will this memorial mean more to you now and in the future? Yes___ No___

6. Do you believe anyone who comes to The Lord's Table should understand what Jesus did for them and what they, personally, are doing as they partake? Yes___ No___

7. Do you believe it is important to make a clear distinction between what is holy and what is unholy? Yes ___ No___

ETERNITY
HEAVEN
OUR GOD IS IN HEAVEN;
HE DOES WHATEVER PLEASES HIM[1]

Most of us have at least a casual thought, from time-to-time, about Heaven. Most of us want to go there and many of us think that everyone will go there, when they leave this earth. We might wonder briefly what Heaven will be like. General thinking seems to waiver among, "I don't know;" "We'll be spirits sitting on a cloud all day, playing a harp;" and "Perhaps we'll come down to haunt people's houses." We really are pretty ignorant about it.

Very few people have actually taken time to look into The Bible to see what God said about it. So, I'm going to tell you what The Bible says and hopefully, you'll become a little more excited about going there.

First, God says,

> Your eye has not seen
> Your ear has not heard
> It hasn't even entered your imagination
> The wonderful things
> God has prepared
> For those who love Him.[2]

That doesn't exactly sound like flitting about as a spirit, sitting on a cloud and strumming a harp, does it? There are Old Testament Scriptures which describe the land God promised His children when they left Egypt. The Promised Land of Canaan is a shadow of what God has for you in Heaven. When the spies returned they reported a land flowing with milk and honey and brought back marvelous fruit. You can read about it in the Book of Numbers, chapter 13.

If that's the kind of land God promised His people on this earth, just imagine what God has prepared for you in Heaven!"

---

[1] Ps. 115:3
[2] 1Cor. 2:9

Jesus is returning soon to take His children home. We don't know the day or the hour but in Matthew 24 He told his disciples what signs to look for. He told them to take a lesson from the "Fig Tree."[3] As soon as its twigs get tender and its leaves come out, you know that summer is near. Even so, when you see all these things come to pass, you know the time is near, even right at the door." He continued, I tell you the truth, this generation (that sees this begin) will certainly not pass away until all these things have happened."

The nation of Israel has always been God's barometer of world events. In 1948, her twigs became tender and she began to put out her leaves.[4] This is significant because it was the fulfillment of the prophecy in Ezekiel 36 and 37. On May 14, 1948, David Ben-Gurion, the Head of the Jewish Agency, proclaimed the State of Israel. Until then the land of Israel was bare and dry like a desert—just as The Old Testament prophets prophesied it would be. After Israel became a state, her land begun to flourish like The Garden of Eden. This, too, was prophesied.[5]

God said the generation that saw the Fig Tree begin to flourish will not pass away until all the things He foretold would happen.[6] Man, according to Scripture has been allotted seventy years—maybe eighty, if he is strong.[7] God tells us to be alert and consider the signs. So, let's consider seventy or eighty years from 1948. That would take us to 2018-2028. I would add that when you see the Fig Tree begin to put out its leaves and the fruit begin to appear and ripen, you know the harvest is near.

We do not know the day nor the hour; but God promises that He will come in the clouds and bring with Him those who have fallen asleep in Him. His bride (the church) will be caught up together with them in the clouds, and so shall we ever be with the Lord.[8]

---

[3] Symbolic of Israel; The Fig Tree Blossoms; Paul Liberman, Messianic Jew; Mt. 24:32-34
[4] Israel declared a state: Midnight, May 14, 1948; US Dept. of State; Gov. History
[5] Jer. 14:1-25:38; Ezk. 36:1-36 (esp. 35)
[6] Mt. 24; 32-35;
[7] Ps. 90:10
[8] 1Th. 4:13-17

In Heaven Jesus will serve us The Marriage Supper of the Lamb,[9] which will include elements of the Last Supper. He will have us recline[10] at table, and dress Himself to serve. Then He will wait on us.[11] At that time, we will see clearly, face-to-face, and we will know and understand everything, just as Jesus does.[12] We will have opportunity to walk and talk with Jesus and see our names in the Book of Life. I don't know if we will recognize that there are names missing…I wonder.

God promises to wipe every tear from our eyes. Perhaps that refers to tears shed because of trials we have come through on earth. Perhaps there will be tears of sorrow for things we could have done for Jesus, but didn't. Perhaps there are words we will wish we had spoken to persuade a friend or relative to get ready for Jesus, but didn't. The Bible doesn't tell us.

Yes, God will wipe away all tears from our eyes.[13] The Bible says that God lists our tears on His scroll and stores our tears in bottles;[14] but it doesn't tell us what will happen to all of these tears once we get to Heaven. I like to think that God will have a big "Get Over It" ceremony in which we all pour our tears into the River of Life. Whatever He chooses, I'm looking forward to it.

Everyone who gets to Heaven will receive the gift of salvation. It doesn't matter if we have lived for Jesus all of our lives or accepted Jesus as we were going through death's door, we all receive the gift of salvation.[15] Salvation would seem to me to be enough; but God promises other rewards, as well.

Rewards God promises: a Prophet's Reward;[16] Righteous Man's Reward;[17] Rewards according to what each of us has done for God;[18] Reward for being persecuted & disgraced for Jesus' sake;[19] Reward for loving our enemies;[20]

---

[9] Lk. 12:35-38 esp. v 37
[10] Signifies rest Mt. 11:28,29
[11] Luke 12: 37;
[12] 1Cor. 13:9-12
[13] Rev. 7:17; 21:4
[14] Ps. 56:8 KJV
[15] Mt 20:1-16
[16] Mt. 10:41,42
[17] Ibid.
[18] Mt. 16:27Rev. 22:12
[19] Lk. 6:21-23; Heb. 11:26
[20] Lk. 6:35

Reward for fire-tested works, which survive;[21] Reward for voluntarily preaching The Gospel;[22] Reward for doing good to God's people;[23] Reward of an inheritance from The Lord;[24] Reward for going in secret to pray to God.[25]

God says that He will take people to Heaven because they have persevered under trial. They kept going when life was not fair and was not easy.[26] They stood for Him no-matter-what. They overcame this world by the blood of The Lamb and by the word of their testimony.[27] Here is some of what Jesus **promises to overcomers**: They will have the right to eat from the Tree of Life and live forever.[28] They will not be hurt at all by the second death.[29] They will eat the hidden manna[30] and receive a white stone with a new name known only to the recipient.[31] God will give them authority over nations[32] and they will rule and reign with Him on this earth. They will receive the Morning Star[33] and walk with Jesus, dressed in white because He counts them worthy.[34] Their names will always be in the Book of Life and they will be acknowledged before God and the angels.[35] They will be kept from the hour of trial that is coming upon the whole earth[36] and they will be a pillar in God's temple[37] never again to leave it. They will wear the name of God and Jesus' new Name[38] and the name of God's city, The New Jerusalem. They will be given the right to sit with Jesus on His throne.

Throughout eternity, we will see God in His human form, as He was when He died for us. We will see the scars in His hands and always remember that we are engraved on the palms of His hands.[39] As all of these promises

---

[21] 1Cor. 3:14
[22] 1Cor. 9:17,18
[23] Eph. 6:7,8
[24] Col. 3:24
[25] Mt. 6:6
[26] Jas. 1:12
[27] Rev. 12:11
[28] Rev.2:7
[29] Rev. 2:11;20:14,15
[30] Rev. 2:17
[31] Rev. 2:17Lp.
[32] Rev.2:26
[33] Rev, 2:28
[34] Ibid Rev.3:4
[35] Rev. 3:5.
[36] Rev. 3:10
[37] Rev. 3:11
[38] Rev. 3:12
[39] Isa. 49:16

are given to the victorious saints, can you imagine the surprise and delight as we run around exploring Heaven; eating the delicious fruit of the Tree of Life and the Hidden Manna. I can imagine there will be quite a gathering around the Tree of Life. I know many people, myself included, who have made appointments with loved ones to have a great reunion there. Well, we don't know exactly what we will do or in what time-frame; but we can trust God that it will be wonderful. No matter what we've come through, Heaven will be cheap enough.

God tells us there will be many crowns distributed in that day. Jesus will give us a Crown of Life;[40] Crown of Beauty;[41] Crown of blessings and vindication;[42] Crown of Everlasting joy;[43] Crown of Glory;[44] Crown of Knowledge;[45] Crown of Righteousness[46] and Crown of Splendor.[47] We will be so overwhelmed and grateful for His wonderful salvation that we will kneel at our Savior's feet and lay our crowns at His throne. In adoration and praise we will worship Jesus, saying:

You are worthy our Lord and God
to receive glory and honor and power for
You created all things[48]and
by Your will they were created and
have their being.[49]

Description of Jesus:
When John saw Jesus, in the vision of Revelation, He looked like a son of man. He was dressed in a robe reaching to His feet, with a golden sash around His chest. His head and hair were white like wool, as white as snow and His eyes were blazing like fire. His feet were like bronze glowing in a furnace and His voice was like the sound of rushing water. In His right hand He held seven stars and out of His mouth came a sharp double-edged

---

[40] Jas. 1:12; Rev. 2:10
[41] Isa. 61:3; 62:3
[42] Ps. 24:5
[43] Isa. 35:10; 51:11
[44] 1Pet. 5:4
[45] Prov. 14:18
[46] 2Tim. 4:8; Rev. 2:10
[47] Prov. 4:9
[48] Heb. 1:9-12; Eph. 3:9; Rev. 4:11
[49] Rev. 4:10,11; Ac. 17:28

sword. His face was like the sun shining in all of its brilliance.[50] He told John, "I am the Living One. I was dead; but behold I am alive forever and ever. I hold the keys of death and Hades. I AM The Alpha and The Omega, The First and The Last. John saw a vision of God on His throne in Heaven and he said He had the appearance of jasper and carnelian

Description of Jesus' Throne:
Righteousness and judgement are the foundations of God's throne; love and faithfulness goes before Him.[51] It is a lofty throne, holy and glorious.[52] John saw a vision of it and said the person sitting on it had the appearance of jasper and carnelian and a rainbow resembling an emerald encircled it.[53] From the throne came flashes of lightning, rumblings and peals of thunder. Before the throne, blazed seven lamps, which are the spirits of God. In the center of the throne, a Lamb, looking as if it had been slain, was standing.[54] The Lamb will be our shepherd and lead us to living water. He will wipe away every tear from our eyes. Before the throne was a sea of glass as clear as crystal. From the throne of God and the Lamb, flowed the water of Life, as clear as crystal. Around the throne were four living creatures with six wings covered all around with eyes of wisdom—even under their wings.

Day and night they never stopped saying,

Holy, Holy, Holy
is The Lord God Almighty.
Who was, and is, and is
to come.[55]

We will be in Heaven, with Jesus for three-and-a-half years, communing with God and worshiping Him. During that time, we will neither marry nor give in marriage. Our highest joy will be to be with Our Lord. The Bible says we will sing a new song, "The Song of Moses and The Lamb".[56] When

---

[50] Rev. 1:13ff
[51] Ps.45:6; 89:14; 93:2
[52] Isa. 63:15
[53] Rev. 4:3
[54] Rev. 5:6
[55] Rev.4:8
[56] Rev. 15:3,4

we sing about salvation, the angels cannot participate; because they don't understand the joy that salvation brings.[57]

You can study more about Heaven and I hope you do. You can read about the Temple, known as the "Tabernacle of The Testimony," and all the wonderful things going on in Heaven. There certainly will not be a dull moment. Be sure you don't miss it! I will close this chapter with,

> To Him who is able to keep us from falling
> and to present us before His glorious throne,
> without fault and with great joy;
> to the only God, our Savior,
> be glory, majesty, power and authority,
> through Jesus Christ our Lord,
> before all ages, now and forevermore![58]
> Come Lord Jesus![59]
> Amen

Segue (for independent study)

God's promise to overcomers is that He will keep them from the "hour of trial that is going to come upon the whole world to test those that are on the earth."[60] This time of trouble will last seven years (you need to choose to study prophetic time). I believe we are nearing the mid-point of that tribulation now. Jesus will remove His ambassadors soon[61]—for ambassadors are always called home prior to war. When He takes us home, The Holy Spirit that dwells within us and has been holding hell in check, will be withdrawn from this earth; and evil will be completely rampant— absolutely out of control. At the end of that time, the saints will return to this earth with Jesus to rule and reign with Him for a thousand years.[62] During the millennial reign of Christ, there will be peace on the earth.

At the beginning of the thousand years, Jesus will seize Satan and bind him with a great chain and throw him into the Abyss; then Jesus will lock and

---

[57] 1Pet 1:12Lp
[58] Jude 24,25
[59] Rev. 22:20
[60] Rev, 3:10
[61] 1Th. 4:16-18
[62] Rev.20:6

seal the Abyss over him, to prevent him from deceiving the nations until the thousand years are ended. After the thousand years, Satan will be set free for a short time.[63]

> So dear to my heart is the promise of God,
> A Home with the pure and blest
> Where earth's weary pilgrims,Strangers here below,
> Will find their eternal rest.
> I'm homesick for Heaven, seems I cannot wait!
> I'm yearning to enter Zion's pearly gate:
> Never a heartache, never a care,
> I long for my Home over there.[64]

---

[63] Rev. 20:2
[64] Homesick for Heaven; Henry de Fluiter; 1950

Heaven Revisited

1. Did you take time to check out the study texts?
   ___All ___Some ___None

2. Are you going to Heaven? Yes___ No___

3. Do you have friends or family who are not ready to meet Jesus?
   Yes___ No___

4. If yes, do you plan to warn them that Jesus is coming soon and to
   get ready? Yes___ No___

5. Have you heard your Pastor or Priest preach about Jesus' soon
   return? Yes ___ No ___

6. Do you believe that it is an important message for this time in
   earth's history? Yes___ No___

7. Do you pray that Jesus comes quickly and soon? Yes___ No___

Amen, Come Lord Jesus![1]

---

[1] Rev. 22:20Lp

HELL

Possibly you wonder why I talk of Heaven, then Hell and finally, The New Earth. Because, that is the order in which The Biblical events unfold.

After the thousand years are ended, Satan is loosed from the Abyss where he was locked and chained. The wicked dead will come to life and Satan will go out to deceive the nations all over the world and gather them together for battle. The numbers are like the sand on the seashore. They march across the earth and surround the people of God in The New Jerusalem. Fire will come down from Heaven and devour them and the devil, who deceived them, will be thrown into the lake of burning sulfur, where the beast and the false prophet already are. They all will be tormented day and night for ever and ever.[1]

God gave an example of Hell's fire when He completely destroyed Sodom and Gomorrah by raining-down, on them, fire and Sulphur. He condemned the cities of Sodom and Gomorrah by burning them to ashes, never to be heard from again. He made them an example of what is going to happen to the ungodly.[2]

Hell is an eternal fire prepared for the devil and his angels.[3] Anyone who worships the beast and his image and receives his mark on the forehead or on the hand will be tormented with burning sulfur in the presence of the holy angels and The Lamb.[4] The righteous will trample down the wicked; they will be ashes under the soles of the saint's feet.[5]

God specifically told us that certain ones will go to Hell:

Anyone who is angry or who engages in name-calling toward a Christian brother or sister,[6]
Anyone with unconfessed sin,[7]

---

[1] Rev. 20:10
[2] 2Pet. 2:6
[3] Mt. 25:41
[4] Rev. 14:9-11
[5] Mal. 4:3
[6] Mt. 5:22
[7] Gen. 18:24; (S&G example of unconfessed sin) Ezk. 33:11-16

Anyone who does not forgive[8]
Priests & teachers who teach untruths: (telling or patterning lies or by failing to speak the truth).[9]

Jesus holds the keys to death and Hades. At the end of the world the sea, death and Hades will give up their dead. The dead both great and small will stand before Christ's White Throne Judgement. Books of life records will be opened and another book, The Book of Life, will be opened. The dead will be judged according to what they have done, as recorded in the books of life records. Then death and Hades will be thrown into The Lake of Fire. The Lake of Fire is the second death. Anyone, whose name is not found written in the Book of Life, will be thrown into The Lake of Fire.[10]

---

[8] Mt. 6:15
[9] 2Pet. 2:1ff; Jude 4-16
[10] Rev. 20:11-15

Hell Revisited

1. Did you take time to check out the study texts?
    ___All ___Some ___None

2. Did you know that the judgement God rained down on Sodom & Gomorrah is an example of His coming judgement and end-of-the-world punishment? Yes___ No___

3. How do you treat your Christian brothers and sisters? _____

    _____

4. Do you ever call them names (even behind their backs)
    Yes___ No___

5. If you are a priest or a pastor, is your message Bible-based and biblically sound? Yes___ No___

    Do you need to pray God to give you biblical sermons
    Yes___ No___

6. If you are a parishioner, does your priest or pastor deal truthfully with you, preaching from The Bible only?
    Yes___ No___ I don't know___

7. Do you love to pray to God in Jesus' Name?
    Yes___ I need to do better___

8. Is there unconfessed sin in your life? Yes ___ No ___

9. Is there anyone you need to forgive? Yes___ No___

The New Earth

In keeping with His promise,
we are looking forward to a new heaven and a new earth,
the home of the righteous.
2 Peter 3:13

Then, I saw a new heaven and new earth;
for the first heaven and the first earth had passed away,
and there was no longer any sea.
Revelation 21:1

After this world is cleansed by fire, God will create a new earth, we will never remember the former earth; it won't even come to mind. The New Earth will be pristine, just as the earth was at creation. We will rejoice over God's creation and the sounds of rejoicing will be heard in the New Jerusalem. We will be a people of joy. Jesus will be there and He will rejoice.

There will never again be the sound of weeping or the voice of crying. Infants will not die and old men will live.[1] There will be no sickness, no pain, no sorrow. Death has been swallowed up in victory![2]

We will build houses and live in them; we will plant gardens and vineyards and eat their fruit. We will never again lose our homes or our wealth.

We will enjoy our beautiful yards, sit under our trees and visit with neighbors. No one will cause us to be afraid. We will thoroughly enjoy the work of our hands. Our seed, both in the garden and in our offspring, will be the blessed of The Lord.

When we call upon The Lord, He will hear and answer us, while we are still speaking. He will be our delight and He will give us the desires of our hearts.

The wolf and the lamb will feed together and the lion will eat straw like the ox. The leopard will lie down with the goat and the calf, the lion and

---

[1] Isa. 65:19-20
[2] 1Cor. 15:54Lp

the yearling will play together; and a little child shall lead them. The infant will play near the hole of the cobra and the young child will put his hand into the viper's nest; dust will be the serpent's food. Nothing will hurt or destroy in all My holy mountain.[3]

In The New Earth, we will worship God on the seventh day Sabbath, the day on which God rested from His creative work. The day that He sanctified and made holy.

From one Sabbath to another and from one new moon to another, all flesh will come to worship before God.[4] Hmmm…I wonder if we will have potlucks! If so, the food will be wonderful and the fellowship will be out of this world!

**In Christ there is no east nor west
In Him no south or north;
But one great fellowship of love
Throughout the whole wide earth.
In Him shall true hearts everywhere
Their high communion find;
His service is the golden cord
Close binding all mankind.
Join hands then, precious ones of faith,
Whatever your race may be.
Who serves my Father as His child is surely kin to me.
In Christ now meet both east and west
In Him meet south and north;
All Christly souls are one in Him
Throughout the whole wide earth.[5]**

---

[3] Isa. 11:6-9; 65:22-25
[4] Isa. 66:23
[5] In Christ There Is No East nor West; Alexander R. Reinagle; 1836

The New Earth Revisited

1. Did you take time to check out the study texts?
   ___All ___Some ___None

2. What did you like best about The Bible's description of The New Earth? _____

   _____

3. Do you plan to live there? Yes___ No___

4. Can you think of friends and relatives whom you want to encourage to be ready to live there? Yes___ No___

5. If yes, make a note of who they are_____

   _____

   _____

The Sabbath

God created[1] this world and everything in it in six literal days. God said "six days," so I believe it. He marked them by the evening (sundown) and the morning (sunrise). By the seventh day, God had completed all of His work, so He rested. God blessed the seventh day and made it holy, because on it He rested from His work of creating.[2]

God commanded the Israelites:

> "Keep the Sabbath day to sanctify it, as the Lord
> thy God hath commanded thee.
> Six days thou shalt labor and do all thy work;
> But the seventh day is the Sabbath of the Lord thy God.
> In it thou shalt not do any work,
> thou, nor thy son, nor thy daughter,
> nor thy manservant, nor thy maidservant,
> nor thine ox nor thy donkey,
> nor thy cattle
> nor the stranger that is within thy gates—
> that thy manservant and maidservant may rest as well as thou.
> And remember that thou wast a servant in the land of Egypt
> and that the Lord thy God brought thee out thence
> Through a mighty hand
> And by a stretched out arm.
> Therefore,
> The Lord thy God
> Commanded thee to keep the Sabbath day.[3]

Today, people worship on various days. Many worship on Saturday, many worship on Sunday.

The council in Jerusalem met, after Gentiles began entering the church, to discuss this matter and seek counsel from The Holy Spirit of Jesus as to what requirements should be placed upon the Gentiles.

---

[1] Gen. 1:1; Heb. 1:10-12
[2] Gen. 2:3
[3] Deut. 5:12-15

The Jews had many requirements such as keeping the seventh-day Sabbath, circumcision, kosher foods, not eating animals cooked in their mother's milk, keeping dishes used for preparing flesh foods, separate from those used to prepare fruits and vegetables, etc. Some of the Jewish believers were attempting to put these same rules, and others, on the gentile believers.

The Jerusalem Council came back with this decision saying, "It seemed good to us and to the Holy Spirit:

"…we should not make it difficult for Gentiles who are turning to God.
Tell them to abstain from food polluted by idols, from
sexual immorality, from the meat of strangled animals
and from blood."[4]

It is true that as the apostles preached, they often preached in the synagogues on the Sabbath and so many of the converts did keep the seventh-day Sabbath. The Apostles, it seems, actually preached The Gospel every day and whenever they got a chance.

It is also true that Emperor Constantine (306-337 A.D), saw visions which moved him to profess Christianity. He was the first pope, who purported to be a Christian—as opposed to pagan. His title was Pontius Maximus. In 321 A.D. he legislated that the day of the sun should be a day of rest for all citizens.[5]

God knew the struggles His children would endure as they sought to honor Him in worship and so He told us all, through the Apostle Paul:

One person considers one day as sacred,
Another considers every day to be alike.
Each of us needs to be convinced in our own mind.
If you regard one day more special
You do so to glorify God.[6]
Do not let anyone judge you
By what you eat or drink

---

[4] Ac. 15:19,20
[5] Codex Justinianus 3.12.2
[6] Rom. 14:5,6

Or with regard to a religious festival
A new moon celebration
or a Sabbath day.
These are only a shadow of things to come.
The real deal is Jesus Christ.[7]

Final thoughts on Sabbath

The day we worship is not important. Worship on Saturday, worship on Sunday, worship every day, if you want to—it doesn't matter. What does matter is that we worship the Lord Jesus with our whole heart. We will worship with our whole heart, if we love the Lord our God with all of our heart and soul and mind.[8]

The Bible tells us the story of Hagar and Sarah, wives of Abraham. By these two women, Abraham had two sons, Ishmael and Isaac. Ishmael was born in the ordinary way; but Isaac was born as the result of a promise. Abraham was one hundred years old and Sarah was ninety when Isaac was born. These two women, Hagar and Sarah represent the Old Covenant and the New Covenant.

The Old covenant was from Mount Sinai, which was the site of the giving of the law. Hagar represents the children of Old Jerusalem. These are children who were born in slavery to the law— slaves to legalism.

Sarah represents the free children born under the New Covenant, children of the New Jerusalem. We are, like Isaac, children of promise. When Isaac was born, the child born in the ordinary way persecuted the son of the promise. God said, "Get rid of the slave woman and her son. They will never share in the inheritance with the free woman's son.[9]

We are all sons and daughters of God,
If we have faith in Jesus Christ.
Being baptized into Christ,

---

[7] Col. 2:16,17
[8] Mt. 22:37-38
[9] Gal. 4:21-31

We have been clothed with Christ.
There is neither Jew, Greek, slave or free;
There is neither male nor female for we are all one in Christ Jesus.
If you belong to Christ,
you are Abraham's seed
And heirs according to the promise.[10]

We are not children enslaved by rules. We worship God in spirit and in truth. Do not allow anyone to look down on your freedom. Do not let anyone judge the day you keep. Teach and encourage one another with all wisdom. Sing songs, hymns and spiritual songs and, as you sing, have gratitude in your hearts. Then, whatever you do, whether singing, speaking or doing, you will bring all glory to God in The Name of Jesus Christ.

In The New Earth, we will worship God on the seventh day Sabbath, the day on which God rested from His creative work. The day that He sanctified and made holy.

From one Sabbath to another and from one new moon to another, all flesh will come to worship before God.[11]

Until that day, whatever day you choose to worship: Worship.

Whatever day you keep: Keep it.

May the Lord bless you and keep you;
May The Lord cause His face to shine upon you
and be gracious unto you
May the Lord lift up His countenance upon you
and give you His peace.[12]

---

[10] Gal 3:26-29
[11] Isa. 66:23
[12] Num. 6:24-26

Sabbath Revisited

1. Did you take time to check out the study texts?
   ___All ___Some ___None

2. Do you know individuals who worship on a day other than the day you worship? Yes___ No___

3. If yes, have you mentally, or verbally, labeled them as strange? Yes___ No___

4. Have you ever had someone attempt to talk you into worshiping on another day? Yes___ No___

5. Have you ever attempted to talk someone else into worshiping on another day? Yes___ No___

6. Do you worship with your whole heart?

7. In The New Earth, everyone will worship together on the same day. Isn't that great?!

Printed in the United States
By Bookmasters